The Healthy Air Fryer Cookbook

for Beginners 2024

1900+ Days Affordable, Flavorful Dishes You Will Love to Master the Art of Air Frying

Michelle D. Thomas

Contents

Chapter 1 Breakfast 1

Air Fried Beef & Vegetable Breakfast Skewers (African-inspired) 1

Air Fried Duck & Hoisin Breakfast Wraps (Chinese-inspired) 1

Air Fried Prosciutto & Melon Bites (Italian-inspired) 1

Air Fried Lamb Kofta & Tzatziki Pita Pockets (Middle Eastern-inspired) 1

Air Fried Pineapple & Coconut French Toast (Tropical-inspired)............................ 2

Air Fried Apple & Cinnamon Oatmeal Cups (European-inspired) 2

Air Fried Berry & Mascarpone Stuffed Crepes (French-inspired)............................ 2

Air Fried Mango & Chia Seed Pudding Parfait (Tropical-inspired) 3

Air Fried Peach & Ricotta Toasts (Mediterranean-inspired) 3

Air Fried Kiwi & Coconut Pancake Bites (Oceanian-inspired)............................... 3

Air-Fried Full English Breakfast... 3

Air-Fried Sausage Rolls 4

Croissant breakfast casserole 4

Breakfast sliders 5

Air-Fried Crumpets... 5

Air-Fried Scotch Eggs.. 5

Chapter 2 Lunch 6

Air Fryer British Fish and Chips 6

Air Fryer Mexican Quesadillas 6

Air Fryer Indonesian Tempeh Satay 6

Air Fryer Australian Meat Pie 6

Air Fryer South African Bunny Chow 7

Air Fryer Italian Caprese Chicken 7

Air Fryer Greek Tzatziki Meatballs 7

Air Fryer Filipino Lumpiang Shanghai 7

Air Fryer Russian Pelmeni.. 7

Vietnamese Banh Mi Sandwiches 8

Quiche Lorraine 8

Falafel 9

Pulled Pork Sandwiches 9

Chapter 3 Diner.. 10

Air Fryer Greek Moussaka... 10

Air Fryer Japanese Teriyaki Chicken 10

Air Fryer South African Bobotie 10

Air Fryer Chilean Pastel de Choclo 11

Air Fryer Italian Osso Buco 11

Air Fryer Thai Basil Chicken (Pad Krapow Gai) 11

Air Fryer Russian Beef Stroganoff...11

Air Fryer Spanish Paella 12

Air Fryer French Ratatouille 12

Air Fryer Lebanese Kibbeh 12

Air Fryer Peruvian Lomo Saltado 13

Air Fryer Moroccan Lamb Tagine 13

Air Fryer German Bratwurst with Sauerkraut 13

Air Fryer Korean Bulgogi Beef...13

Air Fryer Indian Tandoori Chicken 14

Air Fryer Brazilian Pão de Queijo (Cheese Bread) 14

Air Fryer Greek Moussaka...14

Air Fryer Vietnamese Lemongrass Chicken 15

Air Fryer Swedish Meatballs 15

Air Fryer Egyptian Koshari 15

Stew and Dumplings 15

Roast Beef with Yorkshire Pudding 16

Cottage Pie 17

Sunday Roast 17

Chapter 4 Beef, Pork and lamb 18

Air Fryer Caribbean Pork Chops 18

Air Fryer Italian Beef Braciole 18

Air Fryer Vietnamese Lemongrass Pork 18

Air Fryer Moroccan Lamb Tagine 18

Air Fryer Texan BBQ Pork Ribs 18

Air Fryer British Lamb and Mint Burgers 19

Air Fryer Argentinean Beef Empanadas 19

Air Fryer Korean BBQ Beef Ribs 19

Air Fryer Greek Lamb Souvlaki 19

Air Fryer Hungarian Pork Schnitzel 19

Air Fryer Brazilian Picanha Steak 19

Air Fryer Middle Eastern Lamb Kofta 20

Air Fryer Filipino Pork Adobo 20

Air Fryer Turkish Lamb Shish Kebab 20

Air Fryer Polish Pork Cutlets (Kotlety Schabowe) 20

Air-Fried Pork and Cider Casserole ……………………………………………………20

Air-Fried Beef and Broccoli ……………………………………………………………21

Air-Fried Pork Schnitzel Sandwich ……………………………………………………21

Herb-Roasted Rack of Lamb ……………………………………………………………22

Air-Fried Lamb Kebabs with Tzatziki Sauce …………………………………………22

Air-Fried Pork and Sage Meatloaf ……………………………………………………22

Jamaican Beef Patty ……………………………………………………………………23

Jamaican Curry Goat ……………………………………………………………………23

Steak and Kidney Pie …………………………………………………………………24

Roast Pork with Crackling ……………………………………………………………24

Chapter 5 Fish and seafood …………………………………………………… 25

South African Piri Piri Prawns ………………………………………………………25

Turkish Spiced Mackerel with Yogurt Sauce…………………………………………25

Spanish Garlic Shrimp Tapas (Gambas al Ajillo) …………………………………25

Caribbean Coconut Lime Scallops………………………………………………………25

Egyptian Spiced Tilapia with Tahini Drizzle ………………………………………26

New Zealand Green-Lipped Mussel Fritters …………………………………………26

Malaysian Sambal Stingray Packets …………………………………………………26

Canadian Maple-Glazed Salmon Bites ………………………………………………26

Portuguese Clams in Garlic and White Wine…………………………………………27

West African Spicy Prawn Kebabs ……………………………………………………27

Chilean Sea Bass with Pebre Sauce …………………………………………………27

Korean Spicy Octopus Stir-fry (Nakji Bokkeum) Bites ……………………………27

Scottish Smoked Haddock Fishcakes with Tartar Sauce ……………………………28

Air-Fried Baked Stuffed Clams ………………………………………………………28

Air-Fried Fisherman's Pie ……………………………………………………………28

Garlic Butter Shrimp …………………………………………………………………29

Lemon-Herb Grilled Salmon …………………………………………………………29

Smoked Mackerel Pâté …………………………………………………………………29

Air-Fried Cod with Tartar Sauce………………………………………………………30

Baja Fish Tacos with Cilantro Lime Sauce…………………………………………30

Honey Mustard Glazed Salmon ………………………………………………………31

Sesame-Crusted Ahi Tuna ……………………………………………………………31

Spicy Cajun Catfish……………………………………………………………………31

Japanese Miso-Glazed Cod Fillets …………………………………………………32

Mexican Chipotle Lime Grilled Shrimp ………………………………………………32

Chapter 6 Vegetable and Vegetarian ………………………………………… 33

Air Fryer Thai Vegan Pineapple Fried Rice 33

Air Fryer Polish Vegan Pierogi 33

Air Fryer Japanese Vegan Tempura 33

Air Fryer Mexican Vegan Tofu Tacos 33

Air Fryer French Vegan Ratatouille 34

Air Fryer German Vegan Potato Pancakes...34

Air Fryer Moroccan Vegan Chickpea Tagine...34

Air Fryer Australian Vegan Damper Bread 34

Air Fryer Cuban Vegan Black Bean Bowl 35

Air Fryer Kenyan Vegan Sukuma Wiki 35

Air Fryer Greek Vegan Spanakopita Bites...35

Air Fryer Brazilian Vegan Coxinha 35

Air Fryer Spanish Vegan Paella Bites 36

Air Fryer Turkish Vegan Kofte 36

Air Fryer Italian Vegan Eggplant Parmesan 36

Air Fryer Thai Vegan Spring Rolls 36

Air Fryer Lebanese Vegan Falafel 37

Air Fryer Russian Vegan Borscht Bites 37

Air Fryer Japanese Vegan Okonomiyaki 37

Air Fryer German Vegan Potato Pancakes...37

Air Fryer Mexican Vegan Tofu Tacos 38

Air Fryer French Vegan Ratatouille Bites 38

Air Fryer British Vegan "Fish" and Chips 38

Air Fryer Indian Vegan Samosas 38

Air Fryer Caribbean Vegan Jerk Jackfruit Sliders 39

Air Fryer Australian Vegan "Sausage" Rolls 39

Air-Fried Veggie Spring Rolls 39

Air-Fried Stuffed Mushrooms with Spinach and Vegan Chees 40

Chickpea Snack Mix 40

Crispy Air-Fried Eggplant Slices 40

Chapter 7 Sides and appetisers 41

Air Fryer Caribbean Vegan Sweet Potato Fritters 41

Air Fryer Greek Vegan Spanakopita Triangles 41

Air Fryer Brazilian Vegan Coxinha 41

Air Fryer Moroccan Vegan Stuffed Peppers 41

Air Fryer Vietnamese Vegan Spring Rolls 42

Air Fryer Spanish Vegan Patatas Bravas 42

Air Fryer Roasted Pickled Beets 42

Air Fryer Kimchi-Style Brussels Sprouts 42

Air Fryer Pickled Jalapeños with Agave 43

Air Fryer Roasted Pickled Red Onions 43

Air Fryer Crunchy Kimchi Cabbage Wedges 43

Air Fryer Rosemary Garlic Potato Wedges 43

Air Fryer Balsamic Glazed Carrots 44

Air Fryer Herb-Stuffed Mushrooms 44

Air Fryer Crispy Zucchini Fries..44

Air Fryer Roasted Brussels Sprouts with Bacon Bits 44

Cauliflower Buffalo Bites 44

Mini Cornish Pasties 45

Pork Dumplings 45

Double Bean Chilli 46

Mini Chicken Satay Skewers 46

Sweet Potato Fries 46

Mini Spinach and Feta Quiches 47

Creamy Beet Salad 47

Butter-Fried Asparagus 47

Chapter 8 Soups and Stews 48

Air Fryer Moroccan Lentil Soup 48

Air Fryer Hungarian Mushroom Soup 48

Air Fryer Greek Lemon Chicken Soup (Avgolemono) 48

Air Fryer French Bouillabaisse 49

Air Fryer Brazilian Feijoada 49

Air Fryer Japanese Miso Salmon Soup 49

Air Fryer Belgian Beef and Beer Stew 49

Air Fryer Russian Borscht with Beef 50

Air Fryer Peruvian Chicken and Cilantro Soup..50

Air Fryer Korean Spicy Tofu and Seafood Stew (Sundubu Jjigae) 50

Air Fryer Spanish Chorizo and White Bean Stew 51

Air Fryer Moroccan Lamb and Apricot Stew 51

Air Fryer Filipino Pork Sinigang 51

Air Fryer Italian Sausage and Bean Soup 52

Air Fryer Greek Chicken Lemon Soup (Avgolemono) 52

Chapter 9 Snacks 53

Air Fryer Filipino Lumpia (Spring Rolls) 53

Air Fryer Middle Eastern Falafel 53

Air Fryer Indonesian Tempeh Chips 53

Air Fryer South African Biltong 53

Air Fryer Turkish Sigara Böreği (Cheese Rolls) 53

Air Fryer Brazilian Coxinha (Chicken Croquettes) 54

Air Fryer Japanese Korokke (Potato Croquettes) 54

Air Fryer Greek Spanakopita (Spinach Pie) 54

Air Fryer Indian Samosas 54

Air Fryer Spanish Patatas Bravas 55

Air Fryer Italian Arancini (Rice Balls) 55

Air Fryer French Ratatouille Stuffed Mushrooms 55

Air Fryer Korean Tteokbokki (Spicy Rice Cakes).................................55

Air Fryer American Buffalo Cauliflower Bites 55

Air Fryer Peruvian Tequeños (Cheese Sticks) 56

Griddled Aubergine Rounds 56

Courgette Fritters 56

Beignets 57

Blueberry Hand Pies 57

Lemon Bars...57

Mozzarella Sticks 58

Chapter 10 Desserts 59

Air Fryer Turkish Baklava Bites 59

Air Fryer Japanese Mochi Donuts 59

Air Fryer Italian Cannoli Cones...59

Air Fryer French Crème Brûlée Bowls 59

Air Fryer Spanish Churro Bites 60

Air Fryer Australian Lamingtons 60

Air Fryer German Apple Fritters 60

Air Fryer Russian Syrniki (Cheese Pancakes) 60

Air Fryer Moroccan Almond Briouats 60

Air Fryer Peruvian Picarones (Sweet Potato Donuts) 60

Air Fryer Polish Faworki (Angel Wings) 61

Air Fryer Chinese Sesame Balls 61

Air Fryer Egyptian Basbousa (Semolina Cake).....................................61

Air Fryer Belgian Liege Waffles 61

Cinnamon Sugar Doughnut Holes 62

Roasted Beet Chips with Feta Cheese Dip 62

Chapter 1 Breakfast

Air Fried Beef & Vegetable Breakfast Skewers (African-inspired)

Prep Time: 40 minutes (including marination)
Cooking Time: 10 minutes / Servings: 4

Ingredients:
- 300 grams beef cubes
- 1 bell pepper, cut into chunks
- 1 red onion, cut into chunks
- 2 tbsp harissa paste
- 2 tbsp yogurt
- 1 tsp ground cumin
- 1 tsp ground coriander
- Salt and pepper to taste
- Wooden skewers, soaked in water

Instructions:
1. In a bowl, mix harissa paste, yogurt, cumin, coriander, salt, and pepper to form a marinade.
2. Marinate the beef cubes in the mixture for at least 30 minutes.
3. Skewer the marinated beef cubes, bell pepper chunks, and red onion onto the soaked wooden skewers.
4. Preheat the Ninja Air Fryer to 180°C.
5. Place the skewers in the air fryer and cook for 10 minutes or until the beef is cooked to your liking, turning halfway.

Air Fried Duck & Hoisin Breakfast Wraps (Chinese-inspired)

Prep Time: 30 minutes / Cooking Time: 20 minutes / Servings: 4

Ingredients:
- 4 small tortilla wraps
- 300 grams duck breast, thinly sliced
- 4 tbsp hoisin sauce
- 2 spring onions, finely sliced
- 1 cucumber, julienned
- 30 ml sesame oil

Instructions:
1. Rub duck slices with sesame oil and a pinch of salt.
2. Preheat the Ninja Air Fryer to 180°C.
3. Place the duck slices in the air fryer and cook for 15 minutes or until crispy on the outside and tender inside.
4. Warm the tortilla wraps in the air fryer for 2 minutes.
5. Spread hoisin sauce on each wrap, place cooked duck slices, spring onions, and cucumber.
6. Roll up the wraps tightly and serve.

Air Fried Prosciutto & Melon Bites (Italian-inspired)

Prep Time: 10 minutes / Cooking Time: 5 minutes / Servings: 4

Ingredients:
- 12 slices of prosciutto
- 12 melon balls (cantaloupe or honeydew)
- Fresh basil leaves
- Balsamic glaze for drizzling
- Toothpicks

Instructions:
1. Wrap each melon ball with a slice of prosciutto and secure with a toothpick.
2. Garnish each bite with a basil leaf.
3. Preheat the Ninja Air Fryer to 180°C.
4. Place the prosciutto and melon bites in the air fryer and cook for 5 minutes or until the prosciutto is slightly crispy.
5. Drizzle with balsamic glaze before serving.

Air Fried Lamb Kofta & Tzatziki Pita Pockets (Middle Eastern-inspired)

Prep Time: 40 minutes / Cooking Time: 15 minutes / Servings: 4

Ingredients:
- 4 pocket pitas
- 300 grams ground lamb
- 2 tsp ground cumin
- 2 tsp ground coriander
- 1 tsp smoked paprika
- 2 garlic cloves, minced

- Salt and pepper to taste
- 100 grams tzatziki sauce
- Fresh mint leaves
- 30 ml olive oil

Instructions:
1. In a bowl, combine ground lamb, cumin, coriander, paprika, garlic, salt, and pepper. Form into elongated kofta shapes.
2. Preheat the Ninja Air Fryer to 180°C.
3. Brush the kofta with olive oil and place in the air fryer. Cook for 15 minutes or until fully cooked, turning halfway.
4. Warm the pocket pitas in the air fryer for 2 minutes.
5. Stuff each pita pocket with lamb kofta, drizzle with tzatziki sauce, and garnish with fresh mint leaves.

Air Fried Pineapple & Coconut French Toast (Tropical-inspired)

Prep Time: 20 minutes / Cooking Time: 15 minutes / Servings: 4

Ingredients:
- 4 slices of thick-cut bread
- 2 large eggs
- 100 ml coconut milk
- 1 tsp vanilla extract
- 100 grams shredded coconut
- 4 pineapple rings
- Maple syrup for serving
- 30 ml coconut oil

Instructions:
1. Whisk together eggs, coconut milk, and vanilla extract in a bowl.
2. Dip each bread slice into the mixture, ensuring both sides are well-coated, then press into the shredded coconut.
3. Preheat the Ninja Air Fryer to 180°C.
4. Brush each coated bread slice and pineapple ring with coconut oil.
5. Place them in the air fryer and cook for 15 minutes, turning halfway, until the bread is golden and the pineapple is caramelized.
6. Serve the French toast with caramelized pineapple on top and drizzle with maple syrup.

Air Fried Apple & Cinnamon Oatmeal Cups (European-inspired)

Prep Time: 25 minutes / Cooking Time: 20 minutes / Servings: 4

Ingredients:
- 200 grams rolled oats
- 2 apples, finely chopped
- 2 tsp ground cinnamon
- 3 tbsp honey
- 1 large egg
- 200 ml almond milk
- 1 tsp baking powder
- A pinch of salt

Instructions:
1. In a bowl, mix together rolled oats, chopped apples, cinnamon, honey, egg, almond milk, baking powder, and salt.
2. Spoon the mixture into muffin molds.
3. Preheat the Ninja Air Fryer to 180°C.
4. Place the oatmeal cups in the air fryer and cook for 20 minutes or until set and slightly crispy on top.
5. Let them cool slightly before serving.

Air Fried Berry & Mascarpone Stuffed Crepes (French-inspired)

Prep Time: 30 minutes / Cooking Time: 10 minutes / Servings: 4

Ingredients:
- 4 ready-made crepes
- 200 grams mascarpone cheese
- 100 grams mixed berries (blueberries, raspberries, strawberries)
- 3 tbsp powdered sugar
- 1 tsp vanilla extract
- Lemon zest for garnish
- 30 ml butter, melted

Instructions:
1. In a bowl, whisk together mascarpone cheese, powdered sugar, and vanilla extract until smooth.
2. Lay out the crepes and spread the mascarpone mixture in the center of each.
3. Top with mixed berries and fold the crepes into quarters.

4. Brush each crepe with melted butter.
5. Preheat the Ninja Air Fryer to 180°C.
6. Place the stuffed crepes in the air fryer and cook for 10 minutes or until slightly crispy.
7. Garnish with lemon zest and a sprinkle of powdered sugar before serving.

Air Fried Mango & Chia Seed Pudding Parfait (Tropical-inspired)

Prep Time: 10 minutes (plus overnight soaking) / Cooking Time: 10 minutes / Servings: 4

Ingredients:
* 2 ripe mangoes, diced
* 100 grams chia seeds
* 400 ml coconut milk
* 2 tbsp honey
* Granola for layering
* Fresh mint leaves for garnish

Instructions:
1. Mix chia seeds, coconut milk, and honey in a bowl. Refrigerate overnight to allow the chia seeds to expand and form a pudding-like texture.
2. Preheat the Ninja Air Fryer to 180°C.
3. Place the diced mangoes in the air fryer and cook for 10 minutes, until they are caramelized.
4. In serving glasses, layer the chia seed pudding, caramelized mangoes, and granola.
5. Garnish with fresh mint leaves.

Air Fried Peach & Ricotta Toasts (Mediterranean-inspired)

Prep Time: 15 minutes / Cooking Time: 10 minutes / Servings: 4

Ingredients:
* 4 slices of sourdough bread
* 2 ripe peaches, sliced
* 200 grams ricotta cheese
* 2 tbsp honey
* 1 tsp vanilla extract
* Toasted almond slivers for garnish
* 30 ml olive oil

Instructions:
1. Mix ricotta cheese, honey, and vanilla extract in a bowl until smooth.

2. Brush each slice of sourdough bread with olive oil.
3. Preheat the Ninja Air Fryer to 180°C.
4. Place the bread slices and peach slices in the air fryer. Cook for 10 minutes, or until the bread is crispy and the peaches are slightly caramelized.
5. Spread the ricotta mixture on each toast and top with caramelized peach slices.
6. Garnish with toasted almond slivers.

Air Fried Kiwi & Coconut Pancake Bites (Oceanian-inspired)

Prep Time: 20 minutes / Cooking Time: 12 minutes / Servings: 4

Ingredients:
* 150 grams pancake mix
* 2 ripe kiwis, diced
* 50 grams shredded coconut
* 100 ml milk
* 1 large egg
* Maple syrup for drizzling
* 30 ml coconut oil

Instructions:
1. In a bowl, mix together pancake mix, milk, and egg until smooth. Fold in diced kiwis and half of the shredded coconut.
2. Preheat the Ninja Air Fryer to 180°C.
3. Drop spoonfuls of the pancake batter into the air fryer to form small bites.
4. Cook for 12 minutes or until golden and fluffy.
5. Drizzle with maple syrup and sprinkle with the remaining shredded coconut before serving.

Air-Fried Full English Breakfast

Serves 2 / Prep Time: 15 minutes / Cook Time: 23-25 minutes

Ingredients:
* 4 slices of bacon
* 4 sausages
* 2 large eggs
* 4 cherry tomatoes (120g)
* 100g button mushrooms
* 2sices of black pudding
* 2slices of white bread

- Salt and pepper, to taste
- Cooking spray or oil, for air frying

Instructions:
1. Preheat the air fryer to 360°F (180°C) for 5 minutes.
2. Place the sausages in the air fryer basket and cook for 10 minutes, turning them halfway through until they are browned and cooked through. Remove and set aside.
3. Add in the bacon slices immediately into the Air Fryer and cook for 5 minutes until they are crispy. Remove and set aside.
4. Add the cherry tomatoes and mushrooms to the air fryer, season with a pinch of salt and pepper, and air fry for 5 minutes until they are tender. Remove and set aside.
5. Place the black pudding slices in the air fryer and cook for 3 minutes, turning them halfway through until they are heated through and slightly crispy. Remove and set aside.
6. While the black pudding is cooking, make a hole in the center of each slice of bread to accommodate the eggs.
7. Crack an egg into each hole of the bread slices.
8. Spray the air fryer basket with cooking spray or lightly oil it to prevent sticking. Place the bread slices with eggs into the air fryer and cook for 4-5 minutes at 360°F (180°C) until the egg whites are set, and the yolks are still runny.

Air-Fried Sausage Rolls

Serves 2 / Prep Time: 10 minutes / Cook Time: 17-20 minutes

Ingredients:
- 4 pork sausages
- 1 sheet of puff pastry
- 1 egg, beaten
- 1 tablespoon of olive oil
- Salt and pepper, to taste
- Cooking spray or oil, for air frying

Instructions:
1. Preheat your air fryer to 375°F (190°C) for 5 minutes.
2. While the air fryer is preheating, unroll the puff pastry sheet and cut it in half, creating two equal rectangles.
3. Place 2 sausages on each puff pastry rectangle

and roll them up, sealing the edges with a little beaten egg.
4. Brush the top of each sausage roll with beaten egg for a golden finish.
5. Spray the air fryer basket with cooking spray or lightly oil it to prevent sticking. Place the sausage rolls in the air fryer and cook for 12-15 minutes at 375°F (190°C) until they are golden brown and cooked through.

Croissant breakfast casserole

Serves 2 / Prep Time: 15 minutes / Cook time: 30 minutes

Ingredients:
- 2 croissants, torn into pieces
- 2 eggs
- 60ml milk
- 60g shredded cheddar cheese
- 30g cooked and crumbled breakfast sausage
- 30g diced bell peppers
- 30g diced onions
- Salt and pepper to taste

Instructions:
1. In a bowl, whisk together the eggs and milk. Season with salt and pepper.
2. In a separate bowl, combine the torn croissant pieces, cooked sausage, diced bell peppers, diced onions, and half of the shredded cheddar cheese.
3. Pour the egg mixture over the croissant mixture and gently toss to combine.
4. Grease the Ninja Casserole Dish (or an 11 ½ x 7-inch casserole dish). Pour mixture into the dish.
5. Install the wire rack on Level 3. Select AIR ROAST, set temperature to 350°F, and set time to 45 minutes.
6. Press START/STOP to begin preheating.
7. When the unit has preheated, place the casserole dish on the wire rack. Close oven door to begin cooking
8. Sprinkle the remaining shredded cheddar cheese on top.
9. Place the dish in the Air Fry Oven and bake for about 30 minutes or until the casserole is set and the top is golden brown.

Breakfast sliders

Serves 2 / Prep Time: 10 minutes / Cook time: 15 minutes

Ingredients:
* 4 slider buns
* 4 eggs
* 4 slices of cooked bacon
* 2 slices of cheddar cheese
* 1 tablespoon butter
* Salt and pepper to taste

Instructions:
1. Install the wire rack on Level 3. Select AIR ROAST
2. Preheat the Ninja Foodi Digital Air Fry Oven to 350°F (175°C).
3. Split the slider buns and place them in the Air Fry Oven to toast for about 2-3 minutes until lightly golden.
4. In a bowl, whisk the eggs and season with salt and pepper.
5. Heat butter in a skillet over medium heat. Pour in the whisked eggs and scramble until cooked.
6. Place scrambled eggs, bacon, and a slice of cheddar cheese on the bottom bun. Top with the other half of the bun.
7. Place the assembled sliders in the Air Fry Oven for about 5 minutes or until the cheese is melted and the sliders are warmed through.

Air-Fried Crumpets

Serves 2 / Prep Time: 5 minutes / Cook Time: 6 minutes

Ingredients:
* 4 crumpets
* Butter or margarine, for serving (optional)

Instructions:
1. Preheat your air fryer to 375°F (190°C) for 5 minutes.
2. While the air fryer is preheating, lightly butter the crumpets on both sides, if desired.
3. Spray the air fryer basket with cooking spray or lightly oil it to prevent sticking.
4. Place the crumpets in the air fryer basket, ensuring they are not overlapping.
5. Air fry the crumpets for 3 minutes at 375°F (190°C), then flip them over.
6. Continue air frying for another 3 minutes until the crumpets are golden and crispy on the outside.

Air-Fried Scotch Eggs

Serves 2 / Prep Time: 20 minutes / Cook Time: 15 minutes

Ingredients:
* 4 large eggs
* 200g pork sausage meat
* 100g breadcrumbs
* Salt and pepper, to taste
* Cooking spray or oil, for air frying

Instructions:
1. Preheat your air fryer to 375°F (190°C) for 5 minutes.
2. As the air fryer preheats, bring a pot of water to a boil. Carefully add the eggs and boil them for 7 minutes for a slightly runny yolk or 9 minutes for a firmer yolk. Remove the eggs and place them in an ice water bath to cool.
3. Peel the boiled eggs.
4. Divide the sausage meat into 2 equal portions.
5. Flatten each portion of sausage meat in your hand and encase a boiled egg with it, ensuring the egg is fully covered.
6. Roll the sausage-covered egg in breadcrumbs, making sure it's evenly coated.
7. Spray the air fryer basket with cooking spray or lightly oil it to prevent sticking.
8. Place the scotch eggs in the air fryer basket and air fry for 15 minutes at 375°F (190°C) until they are golden brown and the sausage is cooked through.

Chapter 2 Lunch

Air Fryer British Fish and Chips

Prep Time: 20 minutes / Cooking Time: 20 minutes / Servings: 4

Ingredients:
* 4 fish fillets (cod or haddock)
* 200g flour
* 250ml cold sparkling water
* 500g potatoes, cut into chips
* Salt and vinegar to taste
* 2 tbsp vegetable oil

Instructions:
1. Mix flour with sparkling water to create a batter.
2. Dip fish fillets in the batter, ensuring they are well-coated.
3. Toss potato chips in vegetable oil.
4. Air fry battered fish and chips at 190°C for 20 minutes, turning halfway, until golden and crispy.

Air Fryer Mexican Quesadillas

Prep Time: 15 minutes / Cooking Time: 10 minutes / Servings: 4

Ingredients:
* 8 tortillas
* 200g cheddar cheese, grated
* 150g cooked chicken, shredded
* 1 red bell pepper, sliced
* 2 green onions, chopped
* 2 tbsp taco seasoning
* Salsa and sour cream for serving

Instructions:
1. Mix chicken, bell pepper, green onions, and taco seasoning.
2. Place a portion of the chicken mixture on one half of a tortilla, sprinkle cheese on top, and fold the tortilla over.
3. Repeat with remaining tortillas.
4. Air fry at 180°C for 10 minutes or until tortillas are crispy and cheese is melted.

Air Fryer Indonesian Tempeh Satay

Prep Time: 30 minutes (including marination) Cooking Time: 15 minutes / Servings: 4

Ingredients:
* 200g tempeh, cut into cubes
* 100ml peanut sauce
* 2 tbsp soy sauce
* 1 tbsp brown sugar
* 1 clove garlic, minced
* 2 tbsp lime juice
* Bamboo skewers

Instructions:
1. Mix peanut sauce, soy sauce, brown sugar, garlic, and lime juice for the marinade.
2. Marinate tempeh cubes in the mixture for at least 20 minutes.
3. Thread marinated tempeh onto bamboo skewers.
4. Air fry at 190°C for 15 minutes, turning halfway, until the tempeh is golden and slightly crispy.

Air Fryer Australian Meat Pie

Prep Time: 30 minutes / Cooking Time: 25 minutes / Servings: 4

Ingredients:
* 300g beef mince
* 1 onion, chopped
* 2 cloves garlic, minced
* 150ml beef broth
* 2 tbsp tomato paste
* 1 tbsp Worcestershire sauce
* 300g pie dough
* 1 egg, beaten

Instructions:
1. Sauté onion and garlic until translucent. Add beef mince and cook until browned.
2. Stir in beef broth, tomato paste, and Worcestershire sauce. Simmer until a thick gravy forms.
3. Roll out pie dough and line air fryer-safe pie dishes. Fill with beef mixture and cover with

another layer of dough. Seal edges and brush with beaten egg.

4. Air fry at 180°C for 25 minutes or until the crust is golden brown.

Air Fryer South African Bunny Chow

Prep Time: 20 minutes / Cooking Time: 20 minutes / Servings: 2

Ingredients:
- 2 mini loaf breads
- 200g chicken or beef, diced
- 1 onion, chopped
- 2 tbsp curry powder
- 1 tomato, diced
- 250ml chicken or beef broth
- Fresh coriander for garnish

Instructions:
1. Sauté onions until translucent. Add meat and brown.
2. Stir in curry powder, tomatoes, and broth. Simmer until a thick curry forms.
3. Hollow out the centre of the bread loaves. Fill with curry.
4. Air fry the hollowed-out bread tops at 180°C for 5 minutes until crispy.
5. Serve the curry-filled bread with the crispy bread top on the side.

Air Fryer Italian Caprese Chicken

Prep Time: 10 minutes / Cooking Time: 15 minutes / Servings: 4

Ingredients:
- 4 chicken breast fillets
- 150g fresh mozzarella, sliced
- 2 tomatoes, sliced
- Fresh basil leaves
- 4 tbsp balsamic glaze
- Olive oil for brushing
- Salt and pepper to taste

Instructions:
1. Season chicken breasts with salt and pepper.
2. Air fry at 180°C for 10 minutes.
3. Top each chicken breast with mozzarella and tomato slices. Continue air frying for 5 minutes or until the cheese is melted.
4. Garnish with fresh basil and drizzle with

balsamic glaze before serving.

Air Fryer Greek Tzatziki Meatballs

Prep Time: 20 minutes / Cooking Time: 15 minutes / Servings: 4

Ingredients:
- 400g minced lamb or beef
- 1 onion, grated
- 2 cloves garlic, minced
- 1 tsp dried oregano
- 1 tsp dried mint
- Salt and pepper to taste
- 150ml tzatziki sauce for serving

Instructions:
1. Mix minced meat, onion, garlic, oregano, mint, salt, and pepper.
2. Form into golf ball-sized meatballs.
3. Air fry at 190°C for 15 minutes or until meatballs are golden and cooked through.
4. Serve with a generous dollop of tzatziki sauce.

Air Fryer Filipino Lumpiang Shanghai

Prep Time: 25 minutes / Cooking Time: 15 minutes / Servings: 4

Ingredients:
- 200g minced pork
- 100g shrimp, minced
- 1 carrot, finely grated
- 2 cloves garlic, minced
- 2 green onions, finely chopped
- Salt and pepper to taste
- Spring roll wrappers
- Sweet chilli sauce for dipping

Instructions:
1. Mix minced pork, shrimp, carrot, garlic, green onions, salt, and pepper.
2. Place a spoonful of the mixture on each spring roll wrapper and roll tightly.
3. Air fry at 190°C for 15 minutes, turning once, until golden brown.
4. Serve with sweet chilli sauce.

Air Fryer Russian Pelmeni

Prep Time: 45 minutes / Cooking Time: 10 minutes / Servings: 4

Ingredients:
- 300g flour
- 150ml water
- 200g minced beef and pork mix
- 1 onion, finely chopped
- Salt and pepper to taste
- Sour cream for serving

Instructions:
1. Mix flour and water to form a dough. Rest for 20 minutes.
2. Mix minced meat, onion, salt, and pepper for the filling.
3. Roll out the dough thinly and cut out circles. Place a spoonful of filling in the centre of each circle and seal the edges.
4. Air fry at 180°C for 10 minutes or until dumplings are cooked through.
5. Serve with a generous dollop of sour cream.

Vietnamese Banh Mi Sandwiches

Serves: 4 / Prep Time: 20 minutes / Cook time: 15 minutes

Ingredients:
- 4 French baguettes
- 500 g of boneless pork shoulder, sliced thinly
- 2 tbsp. vegetable oil
- 2 cloves garlic, minced
- 1 tbsp. soy sauce
- 1 tbsp. fish sauce
- 1 tbsp. brown sugar
- 1/2 tsp. black pepper
- 64g of mayonnaise
- 1 tbsp. sriracha sauce
- 1 tbsp. lime juice
- 1 tsp. sugar
- 1/2 tsp. salt
- 125 ml of pickled carrots and daikon radish
- 59 ml of chopped fresh cilantro
- 1 jalapeno, sliced
- 4 lettuce leaves

Instructions:
1. Preheat Ninja Dual Zone to Air Fry at 200°C.
2. In a large bowl, combine pork, vegetable oil, garlic, soy sauce, fish sauce, brown sugar, and black pepper. Toss to coat.
3. Place pork in the Ninja Dual Zone and air fry for 12-15 minutes, or until the pork is cooked through and crispy.
4. While the pork is cooking, prepare the sauce by combining mayonnaise, sriracha sauce, lime juice, sugar, and salt in a small bowl. Set aside.
5. Cut the baguettes in half and toast them in the Ninja Dual Zone for 2-3 minutes.
6. Spread the sauce on both sides of the baguette.
7. Add the pickled carrots and daikon radish, chopped cilantro, jalapeno, and lettuce to the sandwich.
8. Add the crispy pork to the sandwich and serve.

Quiche Lorraine

Serves: 6 / Prep Time: 15 minutes / Cook time: 30-35 minutes

Ingredients:
- 1 store-bought pie crust
- 6 large eggs
- 190g of heavy cream
- 250 ml of shredded Gruyere or Swiss cheese
- 6 slices bacon, cooked and crumbled
- 1/2 small onion, finely chopped
- 1/4 teaspoon salt
- 1/4 teaspoon black pepper
- 1/8 teaspoon ground nutmeg

Instructions:
1. Preheat the Ninja Dual Zone to Bake mode at 190°C.
2. Roll out the pie crust and fit it into a 9-inch pie dish. Trim the excess crust and crimp the edges.
3. In a medium bowl, whisk together the eggs, heavy cream, salt, pepper, and nutmeg until well combined.
4. Sprinkle the shredded cheese, cooked bacon, and chopped onion evenly over the bottom of the pie crust.
5. Pour the egg mixture over the filling Ingredients in the pie crust, ensuring they are evenly covered.
6. Place the quiche in the Ninja Dual Zone and bake for 30-35 minutes, or until the centre is set and the top is golden brown.
7. Remove the quiche from the Ninja Dual Zone and let it cool for a few minutes before slicing and serving.

Falafel

Serves: 4 / Prep Time: 15 minutes / Cook time: 15-20 minutes

Ingredients:

- 122 g of dried chickpeas
- 122 g of chopped onion
- 64g fresh parsley leaves
- 64g fresh cilantro leaves
- 2 cloves garlic, minced
- 1 tablespoon flour
- 1 teaspoon baking powder
- 1 1/2 teaspoons ground cumin
- 1 teaspoon ground coriander
- 1/4 teaspoon cayenne pepper
- 1 teaspoon salt
- Oil spray

Instructions:

1. Soak chickpeas in water for at least 12 hours, or overnight. Drain and rinse well.
2. In a food processor, pulse chickpeas until they resemble coarse sand. Add in onion, parsley, cilantro, and garlic, and pulse until finely chopped and mixed with the chickpeas.
3. Transfer the mixture to a large mixing bowl. Add in flour, baking powder, cumin, coriander, cayenne pepper, and salt. Mix well.
4. Preheat the Ninja Dual Zone to air fry at 190°C.
5. Form mixture into small balls, about the size of a golf ball. Spray the basket of the Ninja Dual Zone with oil spray, and place falafel balls in the basket, making sure they are not touching.
6. Air fry falafel for 10 minutes. Open the basket and use tongs to flip the falafel. Air fry for another 5-10 minutes until they are crispy and golden brown.
7. Serve hot with pita bread, hummus, and tzatziki sauce.

Pulled Pork Sandwiches

Serves: 6-8 / Prep Time: 10 minutes / Cook time: 1 hour 30 minutes (plus time for the Ninja Dual Zone to reach pressure)

Ingredients:

- 1500 to 2000 g of pork shoulder
- 1 tbsp. smoked paprika
- 1 tbsp. garlic powder
- 1 tbsp. onion powder
- 1 tbsp. brown sugar
- 1 tsp. salt
- 1/2 tsp. black pepper
- 125 ml apple cider vinegar
- 125 ml ketchup
- 32g brown sugar
- 2 tbsp. Dijon mustard
- 2 tbsp. Worcestershire sauce
- 2 tbsp. honey
- 1 tbsp. smoked paprika
- 1 tbsp. garlic powder
- 1/2 tsp. salt
- 1/2 tsp. black pepper
- 250 ml of water
- For serving:
- Buns or rolls
- Coleslaw

Instructions:

1. In a small bowl, mix the smoked paprika, garlic powder, onion powder, brown sugar, salt, and black pepper. Rub the mixture all over the pork shoulder.
2. In a separate bowl, whisk together the apple cider vinegar, ketchup, brown sugar, Dijon mustard, Worcestershire sauce, honey, smoked paprika, garlic powder, salt, black pepper, and water.
3. Pour the sauce into the Ninja Dual Zone cooking pot.
4. Add the seasoned pork shoulder to the cooking pot and spoon some of the sauce on top.
5. Close the lid and set the Ninja Dual Zone to Pressure Cook mode for 1 hour and 30 minutes.
6. Once the Cooking Time is up, release the pressure manually and carefully remove the pork shoulder from the cooking pot.
7. Using two forks, shred the pork and mix it with the remaining sauce in the pot.
8. Serve the pulled pork on buns or rolls with coleslaw.

Air Fryer Greek Moussaka

Prep Time: 40 minutes / Cooking Time: 45 minutes / Servings: 4

Ingredients:
- 2 large eggplants, sliced
- 400g minced lamb
- 1 onion, chopped
- 2 cloves garlic, minced
- 400g canned tomatoes
- 100ml red wine
- 2 tsp ground cinnamon
- 50g grated Parmesan cheese
- Olive oil for frying
- Salt and pepper to taste
- Béchamel Sauce:
- 50g butter
- 50g flour
- 500ml milk
- 1 pinch nutmeg
- Salt to taste

Instructions:
1. Fry eggplant slices in olive oil until golden on each side. Set aside.
2. Sauté onions and garlic until translucent. Add minced lamb and brown.
3. Add tomatoes, red wine, and cinnamon. Simmer for 20 minutes.
4. For the béchamel sauce, melt butter, stir in flour, and gradually add milk. Stir continuously until thickened. Season with nutmeg and salt.
5. In an air fryer-safe dish, layer eggplant, meat sauce, and béchamel. Repeat layers and top with Parmesan.
6. Air fry at 180°C for 45 minutes or until golden.

Air Fryer Japanese Teriyaki Chicken

Prep Time: 15 minutes (plus marinating time) Cooking Time: 25 minutes / Servings: 4

Ingredients:
- 4 chicken thighs
- 100ml soy sauce
- 50ml mirin
- 50ml sake
- 4 tbsp brown sugar
- 2 cloves garlic, minced
- 1 tbsp ginger, grated
- Spring onions for garnish

Instructions:
1. Mix soy sauce, mirin, sake, brown sugar, garlic, and ginger to form the marinade.
2. Marinate chicken thighs for at least 1 hour.
3. Air fry marinated chicken thighs at 190°C for 25 minutes or until caramelized and cooked through.
4. Garnish with spring onions.

Air Fryer South African Bobotie

Prep Time: 30 minutes / Cooking Time: 40 minutes / Servings: 4

Ingredients:
- 400g minced beef
- 1 onion, chopped
- 2 cloves garlic, minced
- 2 slices of bread, soaked in milk
- 50g raisins
- 2 tbsp curry powder
- 1 tbsp turmeric
- 2 bay leaves
- Salt and pepper to taste
- Custard Topping:
- 2 eggs
- 200ml milk

Instructions:
1. Sauté onions and garlic until translucent. Add minced beef and brown.
2. Squeeze excess milk from the bread and mix it into the meat. Add raisins, curry powder, turmeric, salt, and pepper. Transfer to an air fryer-safe dish.
3. Whisk eggs and milk together and pour over the meat. Place bay leaves on top.
4. Air fry at 180°C for 40 minutes or until the custard is set and golden.

Air Fryer Chilean Pastel de Choclo

Prep Time: 40 minutes / Cooking Time: 45 minutes / Servings: 4

Ingredients:
- 200g minced beef
- 2 chicken breasts, cooked and shredded
- 1 onion, chopped
- 2 cloves garlic, minced
- 4 cups of corn kernels
- 2 tbsp sugar
- 2 tbsp butter
- 2 hard-boiled eggs, sliced
- 10 black olives
- 1 tbsp ground cumin
- Olive oil for frying
- Salt and pepper to taste

Instructions:
1. Sauté onions and garlic in olive oil. Add minced beef, cumin, salt, and pepper. Cook until browned.
2. Blend corn kernels with butter until a paste forms.
3. In an air fryer-safe dish, layer beef mixture, shredded chicken, egg slices, and olives. Top with the corn paste.
4. Sprinkle sugar on top.
5. Air fry at 180°C for 45 minutes or until the top is golden and caramelized.

Air Fryer Italian Osso Buco

Prep Time: 30 minutes / Cooking Time: 50 minutes / Servings: 4

Ingredients:
- 4 veal shanks
- 1 onion, chopped
- 2 carrots, diced
- 2 celery stalks, diced
- 3 cloves garlic, minced
- 400g canned tomatoes
- 200ml white wine
- 2 tbsp olive oil
- 2 bay leaves
- Salt and pepper to taste
- Fresh parsley and lemon zest for garnish

Instructions:
1. Brown veal shanks in olive oil. Set aside.
2. Sauté onions, carrots, celery, and garlic until softened.
3. Add tomatoes, white wine, bay leaves, salt, and pepper. Return the veal shanks to the pan and let it simmer until tender.
4. Transfer to an air fryer-safe dish and air fry at 180°C for 50 minutes.
5. Garnish with a mix of chopped parsley and lemon zest.

Air Fryer Thai Basil Chicken (Pad Krapow Gai)

Prep Time: 15 minutes / Cooking Time: 20 minutes / Servings: 4

Ingredients:
- 400g chicken breast, minced
- 3 cloves garlic, minced
- 3 bird's eye chilies, minced
- 2 tbsp fish sauce
- 1 tbsp soy sauce
- 1 tsp sugar
- 2 cups Thai basil leaves
- 2 tbsp vegetable oil

Instructions:
1. Heat oil in a pan and sauté garlic and chilies until fragrant.
2. Add minced chicken and cook until browned.
3. Stir in fish sauce, soy sauce, and sugar. Cook for another 5 minutes.
4. Add Thai basil leaves and stir until wilted.
5. Transfer to an air fryer-safe dish and air fry at 180°C for 20 minutes.

Air Fryer Russian Beef Stroganoff

Prep Time: 20 minutes / Cooking Time: 30 minutes / Servings: 4

Ingredients:
- 400g beef tenderloin, sliced into strips
- 1 onion, thinly sliced
- 200g mushrooms, sliced
- 200ml beef broth
- 100ml sour cream
- 2 tbsp butter
- 2 tbsp flour
- Salt and pepper to taste

- Fresh dill for garnish

Instructions:
1. Melt butter in a pan and sauté onions until translucent. Add beef strips and brown on all sides.
2. Stir in mushrooms and cook until softened.
3. Sprinkle flour over the mixture and stir, then pour in beef broth. Let it simmer until thickened.
4. Remove from heat and stir in sour cream. Season with salt and pepper.
5. Transfer to an air fryer-safe dish and air fry at 180°C for 30 minutes.
6. Garnish with fresh dill.

Air Fryer Spanish Paella

Prep Time: 30 minutes / Cooking Time: 40 minutes / Servings: 4

Ingredients:
- 200g Arborio rice
- 200g chicken thighs, cubed
- 100g shrimp, peeled and deveined
- 100g mussels, cleaned
- 1 red bell pepper, sliced
- 1 onion, chopped
- 2 cloves garlic, minced
- 400ml chicken broth
- 100ml white wine
- 1 tsp saffron threads
- 2 tbsp olive oil
- Salt and pepper to taste
- Fresh parsley and lemon wedges for garnish

Instructions:
1. Heat olive oil in a pan and sauté onions, garlic, and bell pepper until softened.
2. Add chicken thighs and cook until browned.
3. Stir in rice and saffron threads, then pour in white wine. Let it simmer until reduced by half.
4. Add chicken broth and let the rice cook until almost done.
5. Add shrimp and mussels and cover until seafood is cooked.
6. Transfer to an air fryer-safe dish and air fry at 180°C for 40 minutes.
7. Garnish with fresh parsley and lemon wedges.

Air Fryer French Ratatouille

Prep Time: 20 minutes / Cooking Time: 35 minutes / Servings: 4

Ingredients:
- 1 eggplant, diced
- 1 zucchini, diced
- 1 red bell pepper, diced
- 1 onion, chopped
- 2 cloves garlic, minced
- 400g canned tomatoes
- 2 tbsp olive oil
- 1 tsp dried thyme
- Salt and pepper to taste
- Fresh basil for garnish

Instructions:
1. Heat olive oil in a pan and sauté onions and garlic until translucent.
2. Add eggplant, zucchini, and bell pepper. Cook until softened.
3. Stir in tomatoes and thyme. Let it simmer until vegetables are tender.
4. Season with salt and pepper.
5. Transfer to an air fryer-safe dish and air fry at 180°C for 35 minutes.
6. Garnish with fresh basil.

Air Fryer Lebanese Kibbeh

Prep Time: 30 minutes / Cooking Time: 25 minutes / Servings: 4

Ingredients:
- 200g ground lamb
- 100g bulgur wheat, soaked and drained
- 1 onion, finely chopped
- 2 cloves garlic, minced
- 2 tsp ground cumin
- 1 tsp ground allspice
- 2 tbsp olive oil
- Salt and pepper to taste
- Fresh mint for garnish

Instructions:
1. Mix ground lamb, bulgur wheat, onion, garlic, cumin, allspice, salt, and pepper in a bowl.
2. Shape the mixture into oval balls.
3. Brush each kibbeh with olive oil.
4. Air fry at 190°C for 25 minutes or until crispy

and golden.

5. Garnish with fresh mint.

Air Fryer Peruvian Lomo Saltado

Prep Time: 20 minutes / Cooking Time: 30 minutes / Servings: 4

Ingredients:

- 400g beef tenderloin, sliced
- 1 red onion, sliced
- 1 tomato, sliced
- 2 cloves garlic, minced
- 3 yellow chili peppers, sliced
- 3 tbsp soy sauce
- 2 tbsp vinegar
- 2 tbsp vegetable oil
- Salt and pepper to taste
- Fresh cilantro for garnish

Instructions:

1. Heat oil in a pan and sauté garlic until fragrant. Add beef slices and brown.
2. Add onions, tomatoes, and chili peppers. Stir-fry for a few minutes.
3. Pour in soy sauce and vinegar. Cook until beef is done.
4. Season with salt and pepper.
5. Transfer to an air fryer-safe dish and air fry at 180°C for 30 minutes.
6. Garnish with fresh cilantro.

Air Fryer Moroccan Lamb Tagine

Prep Time: 25 minutes / Cooking Time: 45 minutes / Servings: 4

Ingredients:

- 400g lamb shoulder, cubed
- 1 onion, finely chopped
- 2 cloves garlic, minced
- 100g dried apricots, chopped
- 50g toasted almonds
- 2 tsp ground cumin
- 2 tsp ground coriander
- 1 tsp ground cinnamon
- 1 tsp ground ginger
- 400ml chicken stock
- 2 tbsp olive oil
- Salt and pepper to taste

- Fresh coriander for garnish

Instructions:

1. In a pan, heat olive oil and brown the lamb cubes.
2. Add onions and garlic, sautéing until translucent.
3. Stir in the spices, ensuring the meat is well-coated.
4. Add dried apricots, almonds, and chicken stock.
5. Transfer the mixture to an air fryer-safe dish and air fry at 160°C for 45 minutes or until the lamb is tender.
6. Garnish with fresh coriander.

Air Fryer German Bratwurst with Sauerkraut

Prep Time: 15 minutes / Cooking Time: 25 minutes / Servings: 4

Ingredients:

- 4 Bratwurst sausages
- 400g sauerkraut, drained
- 1 onion, thinly sliced
- 1 apple, grated
- 200ml beer (optional)
- 2 tbsp vegetable oil
- Salt and pepper to taste
- Mustard for serving

Instructions:

1. In a pan, heat oil and brown the Bratwurst sausages.
2. Add onions, sautéing until translucent.
3. Stir in grated apple and sauerkraut.
4. If using, pour in the beer and let simmer for a few minutes.
5. Transfer the sausages and sauerkraut mixture to an air fryer-safe dish and air fry at 180°C for 25 minutes.
6. Serve with mustard on the side.

Air Fryer Korean Bulgogi Beef

Prep Time: 20 minutes (plus marinating time) Cooking Time: 20 minutes / Servings: 4

Ingredients:

- 400g beef sirloin, thinly sliced
- 100ml soy sauce
- 50ml mirin

- 2 tbsp brown sugar
- 3 cloves garlic, minced
- 1 small pear, grated
- 2 tbsp sesame oil
- 1 tbsp toasted sesame seeds
- 2 green onions, chopped

Instructions:
1. Combine soy sauce, mirin, brown sugar, garlic, pear, and sesame oil to create the marinade.
2. Marinate beef slices for at least 2 hours.
3. Air fry marinated beef at 190°C for 20 minutes or until caramelized.
4. Garnish with sesame seeds and green onions.

Air Fryer Indian Tandoori Chicken

Prep Time: 25 minutes (plus marinating time)
Cooking Time: 30 minutes / Servings: 4

Ingredients:
- 4 chicken legs
- 200ml yogurt
- 2 tbsp lemon juice
- 3 cloves garlic, minced
- 1 tbsp ginger, grated
- 2 tsp garam masala
- 1 tsp turmeric
- 1 tsp cayenne pepper
- 1 tsp paprika
- Salt to taste
- Fresh cilantro for garnish

Instructions:
1. Mix yogurt, lemon juice, garlic, ginger, and spices in a bowl.
2. Marinate chicken legs in the mixture for at least 4 hours.
3. Air fry marinated chicken at 190°C for 30 minutes or until browned and cooked through.
4. Garnish with fresh cilantro.

Air Fryer Brazilian Pão de Queijo (Cheese Bread)

Prep Time: 20 minutes / Cooking Time: 25 minutes / Servings: 4

Ingredients:
- 250g tapioca flour
- 120ml milk

- 60g butter
- 1 tsp salt
- 150g Parmesan cheese, grated
- 2 beaten eggs

Instructions:
1. In a saucepan, combine milk, butter, and salt. Stir occasionally until the milk is hot and the butter is melted.
2. Slowly add tapioca flour, stirring constantly until thoroughly mixed.
3. Remove from heat and let rest for 15 minutes.
4. Add cheese and beaten eggs. Mix until smooth.
5. Shape the dough into balls and place them on an air fryer-safe tray.
6. Air fry at 190°C for 25 minutes or until lightly golden.

Air Fryer Greek Moussaka

Prep Time: 40 minutes / Cooking Time: 50 minutes / Servings: 4

Ingredients:
- 2 large eggplants, sliced
- 400g ground lamb
- 1 onion, chopped
- 3 cloves garlic, minced
- 400g canned tomatoes
- 2 tbsp olive oil
- 1 tsp cinnamon
- 50g grated Parmesan
- Salt and pepper to taste
- Béchamel Sauce:
- 50g butter
- 50g flour
- 500ml milk
- 100g feta cheese, crumbled
- 1 egg yolk

Instructions:
1. Sauté onions and garlic in olive oil. Add ground lamb, cook until browned.
2. Stir in tomatoes, cinnamon, salt, and pepper. Simmer for 20 minutes.
3. For the béchamel sauce, melt butter, stir in flour, and gradually add milk. Whisk continuously until thickened. Off the heat, stir in feta and egg yolk.
4. Layer the bottom of an air fryer-safe dish with

eggplant slices, followed by the lamb mixture, and top with béchamel sauce. Sprinkle with Parmesan.

5. Air fry at 180°C for 50 minutes or until golden brown.

Air Fryer Vietnamese Lemongrass Chicken

Prep Time: 30 minutes (plus marinating time)
Cooking Time: 25 minutes / Servings: 4

Ingredients:

* 4 chicken thighs
* 2 stalks lemongrass, finely chopped
* 3 cloves garlic, minced
* 2 tbsp fish sauce
* 1 tbsp soy sauce
* 2 tbsp honey
* 1 tbsp vegetable oil
* Salt and pepper to taste

Instructions:

1. Mix all Ingredients (except chicken) to create the marinade.
2. Marinate chicken thighs for at least 2 hours.
3. Air fry marinated chicken at 190°C for 25 minutes or until fully cooked.

Air Fryer Swedish Meatballs

Prep Time: 30 minutes / Cooking Time: 20 minutes / Servings: 4

Ingredients:

* 400g ground beef
* 100g breadcrumbs
* 1 egg
* 1 onion, finely chopped
* 250ml beef broth
* 150ml heavy cream
* 2 tbsp butter
* 2 tbsp flour
* Salt, pepper, and nutmeg to taste
* Fresh parsley for garnish

Instructions:

1. Mix beef, breadcrumbs, egg, onion, salt, pepper, and nutmeg. Form into small meatballs.
2. Air fry meatballs at 190°C for 15 minutes or

until browned.

3. For the gravy, melt butter, stir in flour, and gradually add beef broth and cream. Simmer until thickened.
4. Add meatballs to the gravy and cook for an additional 5 minutes.
5. Garnish with fresh parsley.

Air Fryer Egyptian Koshari

Prep Time: 35 minutes / Cooking Time: 30 minutes / Servings: 4

Ingredients:

* 100g rice
* 100g lentils
* 100g macaroni
* 1 onion, thinly sliced
* 400g canned tomatoes
* 2 cloves garlic, minced
* 1 tsp cumin
* 1 tsp paprika
* 2 tbsp vinegar
* 2 tbsp vegetable oil
* Salt and pepper to taste

Instructions:

1. Cook rice, lentils, and macaroni separately as per package Instructions.
2. Fry onion slices in oil until crispy and set aside for garnish.
3. For the sauce, sauté garlic, add tomatoes, cumin, paprika, vinegar, salt, and pepper. Simmer until thickened.
4. In an air fryer-safe dish, layer rice, lentils, and macaroni. Top with the spicy tomato sauce.
5. Air fry at 180°C for 30 minutes.
6. Garnish with crispy onions.

Stew and Dumplings

Serves: 4-6 / Prep Time: 20 minutes / Cook time: 50 minutes

Ingredients:

* 1000 g beef stew meat, cut into 1-inch pieces
* 2 tablespoons all-purpose flour
* 2 tablespoons olive oil
* 1 onion, chopped

- 3 garlic cloves, minced
- 540 g of beef broth
- 256g of chopped carrots
- 256g of chopped celery
- 1 teaspoon dried thyme
- 1 bay leaf
- Salt and pepper to taste
- 128g all-purpose flour
- 2 teaspoons baking powder
- 1/2 teaspoon salt
- 64g milk
- 2 tablespoons butter, melted

Instructions:

1. In a large bowl, toss the beef stew meat with 2 tablespoons of flour until coated.
2. Set the Ninja Dual Zone to Air Fry mode and preheat to 190°C.
3. Add the olive oil to the inner pot and wait for it to get hot.
4. Add the coated beef to the pot and cook until browned on all sides, about 5 minutes.
5. Add the chopped onion and garlic and cook for another 2-3 minutes.
6. Pour in the beef broth and add the chopped carrots, celery, thyme, bay leaf, salt, and pepper.
7. stir everything and close the lid.
8. Set the Ninja Dual Zone to Stew mode and cook for 30 minutes.
9. While the stew is cooking, make the dumplings. In a medium bowl, mix the flour, baking powder, and salt.
10. Add the milk and melted butter and mix until just combined.
11. Once the stew has finished cooking, open the lid and drop spoonfuls of the dumpling batter onto the surface of the stew.
12. Close the lid and set the Ninja Dual Zone to Air Fry mode at 190°C. Cook for another 15-20 minutes or until the dumplings are cooked through and golden brown.
13. Serve the stew and dumplings hot and enjoy!

Roast Beef with Yorkshire Pudding

Serves: 6-8 / Prep Time: 10 minutes / Cook time: 1 hour 15 minutes

Ingredients:
- 408 g beef roast
- Salt and pepper to taste
- 1 tbsp olive oil
- 1 onion, sliced
- 3 garlic cloves, minced
- 128g beef broth
- 125 ml of red wine
- 1 tbsp Worcestershire sauce
- 1 tsp dried thyme
- 1/2 tsp dried rosemary
- 2 tbsp butter
- 2 tbsp all-purpose flour
- 170 g of milk
- 2 eggs
- 128g all-purpose flour
- 1/2 tsp salt
- 250 ml of vegetable oil

Instructions:

1. Preheat the Ninja Dual Zone to Air Fry mode at 190°C.
2. Season the beef roast with salt and pepper.
3. Heat the olive oil in a large skillet over medium-high heat. Add the beef and sear on all sides until browned, about 4-5 minutes per side.
4. Transfer the beef to the Ninja Dual Zone basket and place it in the Air Fryer.
5. In the same skillet, add the sliced onions and garlic and cook until tender, about 3-4 minutes.
6. Add the beef broth, red wine, Worcestershire sauce, thyme, and rosemary to the skillet and stir to combine.
7. Pour the mixture over the beef in the Air Fryer basket.
8. Air Fry for 50-60 minutes or until the beef is cooked to your desired level of doneness.
9. In a separate bowl, whisk together the flour, milk, and eggs until smooth.
10. Add the salt and continue to whisk until the mixture is well combined.
11. Heat the vegetable oil in a 9-inch baking dish until hot.
12. Pour the batter into the baking dish and bake in the Air Fryer at 190°C for 20-25 minutes, or until the Yorkshire pudding is puffed and

golden brown.

13. In a small saucepan, melt the butter over medium heat. Add the flour and whisk until smooth.

14. Gradually add the beef broth mixture from the Air Fryer to the saucepan, whisking constantly, until the gravy thickens.

15. Serve the roast beef with the Yorkshire pudding and gravy on the side. Enjoy!

Cottage Pie

Serves: 6 / Prep Time: 15 minutes / Cook time: 25 minutes

Ingredients:
* 500 g ground beef
* 1 onion, diced
* 2 cloves garlic, minced
* 2 medium carrots, diced
* 1 tbsp tomato paste
* 1 tbsp Worcestershire sauce
* 128g beef broth
* 2 tbsp cornstarch
* 1 tsp dried thyme
* 1 tsp dried rosemary
* Salt and pepper, to taste
* 408 g of mashed potatoes
* 64g shredded cheddar cheese

Instructions:
1. Preheat the Ninja Dual Zone to the bake mode at 190°C.
2. In a large skillet, cook the ground beef over medium-high heat until browned, stirring occasionally. Drain any excess fat.
3. Add the onion, garlic, and carrots to the skillet and sauté until the vegetables are tender, about 5 minutes.
4. Stir in the tomato paste, Worcestershire sauce, beef broth, cornstarch, thyme, rosemary, salt, and pepper. Bring the mixture to a boil and then reduce the heat and let it simmer for 5-10 minutes until the sauce has thickened.
5. Transfer the beef mixture to a 9x13-inch baking dish. Spread the mashed potatoes over the top of the beef mixture, using a spatula to create an even layer.

6. Sprinkle the shredded cheddar cheese over the top of the mashed potatoes.
7. Place the baking dish in the Ninja Dual Zone and bake for 20-25 minutes until the cheese is melted and bubbly.
8. Serve hot and enjoy!

Sunday Roast

Serves: 4-6 / Prep Time: 10 minutes / Cook time: 1 hour and 30 minutes

Ingredients:
* 1500 g beef roast
* 1 tablespoon olive oil
* 1 teaspoon salt
* 1/2 teaspoon black pepper
* 1 teaspoon garlic powder
* 1 teaspoon dried rosemary
* 1 teaspoon dried thyme
* 1 onion, chopped
* 2 carrots, chopped
* 2 stalks of celery, chopped
* 128g beef broth

Instructions:
1. Preheat the Ninja Dual Zone to 190°C.
2. In a small bowl, mix the salt, black pepper, garlic powder, rosemary, and thyme.
3. Rub the olive oil all over the beef roast, and then sprinkle the seasoning mixture on all sides of the roast.
4. Place the chopped onion, carrots, and celery in the bottom of the Ninja Dual Zone Ninja Dual.
5. Place the seasoned beef roast on top of the vegetables.
6. Pour the beef broth over the roast.
7. Use the Ninja Dual setting to set the Ninja Dual Zone to Roast, and cook for 1 hour and 30 minutes, or until the internal temperature of the roast reaches 57°C for medium-rare or 62°C for medium.
8. Let the roast rest for 10-15 minutes before slicing and serving with the cooked vegetables and any desired sides.

Air Fryer Caribbean Pork Chops

Prep Time: 15 minutes / Cooking Time: 14 minutes / Servings: 4

Ingredients:
- 4 pork chops
- 2 tbsp jerk seasoning
- 1 tbsp lime juice
- 2 cloves garlic, minced
- Salt to taste

Instructions:
1. Rub the pork chops with jerk seasoning, lime juice, garlic, and salt.
2. Air fry at 190°C for 14 minutes, flipping halfway.
3. Serve with mango salsa on the side.

Air Fryer Italian Beef Braciole

Prep Time: 20 minutes / Cooking Time: 15 minutes / Servings: 4

Ingredients:
- 4 thin beef steaks
- 100g grated Parmesan cheese
- 2 cloves garlic, minced
- 2 tbsp chopped fresh basil
- Salt and pepper to taste
- 4 toothpicks or kitchen twine

Instructions:
1. Lay out each steak, season with salt and pepper.
2. Sprinkle with Parmesan, garlic, and basil.
3. Roll up each steak and secure with toothpick or twine.
4. Air fry at 180°C for 15 minutes, turning halfway.

Air Fryer Vietnamese Lemongrass Pork

Prep Time: 25 minutes (plus marinating time) Cooking Time: 12 minutes / Servings: 4

Ingredients:
- 400g pork belly, thinly sliced
- 2 stalks lemongrass, finely minced
- 2 tbsp fish sauce
- 1 tbsp honey
- 2 cloves garlic, minced
- 1 red chili, finely chopped

Instructions:
1. Mix all the marinade Ingredients and marinate the pork slices for at least 2 hours.
2. Air fry at 190°C for 12 minutes, flipping once.

Air Fryer Moroccan Lamb Tagine

Prep Time: 20 minutes / Cooking Time: 20 minutes / Servings: 4

Ingredients:
- 400g lamb chunks
- 2 tsp ground cumin
- 2 tsp ground coriander
- 1 tsp ground cinnamon
- 1 tbsp olive oil
- 2 cloves garlic, minced
- 100g dried apricots, halved
- Salt to taste

Instructions:
1. Mix lamb with spices, olive oil, garlic, and salt.
2. Air fry at 160°C for 20 minutes, adding apricots halfway.

Air Fryer Texan BBQ Pork Ribs

Prep Time: 15 minutes / Cooking Time: 25 minutes / Servings: 4

Ingredients:
- 4 pork rib portions
- 3 tbsp BBQ seasoning
- 2 tbsp brown sugar
- 1 tbsp smoked paprika
- Salt to taste

Instructions:
1. Mix BBQ seasoning, brown sugar, paprika, and salt.
2. Rub onto the pork ribs, ensuring an even coat.
3. Air fry at 175°C for 25 minutes, turning once.

Air Fryer British Lamb and Mint Burgers

Prep Time: 20 minutes / Cooking Time: 12 minutes / Servings: 4

Ingredients:
- 400g minced lamb
- 2 tbsp fresh mint, chopped
- 1 egg, beaten
- Salt and pepper to taste
- 4 burger buns

Instructions:
1. Mix lamb, mint, egg, salt, and pepper.
2. Shape into burgers and air fry at 190°C for 12 minutes, flipping once.
3. Serve in buns with lettuce and a minty yogurt sauce.

Air Fryer Argentinean Beef Empanadas

Prep Time: 30 minutes / Cooking Time: 15 minutes / Servings: 4

Ingredients:
- 200g minced beef
- 1 onion, finely chopped
- 2 boiled eggs, chopped
- 2 tbsp chopped olives
- 1 tsp ground cumin
- 1 pack empanada wrappers
- Salt to taste

Instructions:
1. Cook beef with onions, cumin, and salt until browned. Mix in eggs and olives.
2. Fill empanada wrappers with the mixture and fold, sealing edges.

Air Fryer Korean BBQ Beef Ribs

Prep Time: 20 minutes (plus marinating time) Cooking Time: 18 minutes / Servings: 4

Ingredients:
- 4 beef rib portions
- 3 tbsp soy sauce
- 2 tbsp brown sugar
- 1 tbsp sesame oil
- 2 cloves garlic, minced

- 1 small pear, grated

Instructions:
1. Mix all the marinade Ingredients and marinate the beef ribs for at least 3 hours.
2. Air fry at 180°C for 18 minutes, turning once.

Air Fryer Greek Lamb Souvlaki

Prep Time: 25 minutes (plus marinating time) Cooking Time: 15 minutes / Servings: 4

Ingredients:
- 400g lamb chunks
- 2 tbsp olive oil
- 1 tbsp lemon juice
- 2 cloves garlic, minced
- 1 tsp dried oregano
- Salt to taste

Instructions:
1. Mix all Ingredients and marinate the lamb for at least 2 hours.
2. Skewer the lamb chunks and air fry at 190°C for 15 minutes, turning once.

Air Fryer Hungarian Pork Schnitzel

Prep Time: 20 minutes / Cooking Time: 14 minutes / Servings: 4

Ingredients:
- 4 pork cutlets
- 1 cup breadcrumbs
- 1 egg, beaten
- 1 tsp paprika
- Salt and pepper to taste

Instructions:
1. Season pork cutlets with salt, pepper, and paprika.
2. Dip in beaten egg and coat with breadcrumbs.
3. Air fry at 190°C for 14 minutes, flipping halfway.

Air Fryer Brazilian Picanha Steak

Prep Time: 10 minutes / Cooking Time: 15 minutes / Servings: 4

Ingredients:
- 500g picanha steak

- 2 tbsp coarse sea salt
- 1 tbsp olive oil

Instructions:
1. Rub the picanha steak with olive oil and sea salt.
2. Air fry at 200°C for 15 minutes, flipping halfway for a medium-rare finish.
3. Let it rest for a few minutes before slicing.

Air Fryer Middle Eastern Lamb Kofta

Prep Time: 20 minutes / Cooking Time: 12 minutes / Servings: 4

Ingredients:
- 400g minced lamb
- 1 onion, finely chopped
- 2 cloves garlic, minced
- 2 tsp ground cumin
- 2 tsp ground coriander
- Salt and pepper to taste

Instructions:
1. Mix all Ingredients thoroughly.
2. Shape into elongated meatballs and air fry at 190°C for 12 minutes, turning once.

Air Fryer Filipino Pork Adobo

Prep Time: 15 minutes (plus marinating time) Cooking Time: 18 minutes / Servings: 4

Ingredients:
- 400g pork belly chunks
- 4 cloves garlic, minced
- 1/2 cup soy sauce
- 1/4 cup vinegar
- 1 tsp black peppercorns
- 2 bay leaves

Instructions:
1. Marinate pork chunks with all Ingredients for at least 2 hours.
2. Air fry at 180°C for 18 minutes, turning once.

Air Fryer Turkish Lamb Shish Kebab

Prep Time: 25 minutes (plus marinating time) Cooking Time: 15 minutes / Servings: 4

Ingredients:
- 400g lamb chunks
- 2 tbsp yogurt
- 1 tbsp olive oil
- 1 tsp ground paprika
- 1 tsp ground cumin
- Salt and pepper to taste

Instructions:
1. Mix all Ingredients and marinate the lamb for at least 4 hours.
2. Skewer the lamb chunks and air fry at 190°C for 15 minutes, turning once.

Air Fryer Polish Pork Cutlets (Kotlety Schabowe)

Prep Time: 20 minutes / Cooking Time: 14 minutes / Servings: 4

Ingredients:
- 4 pork cutlets
- 1 cup breadcrumbs
- 1 egg, beaten
- 2 tbsp flour
- Salt and pepper to taste

Instructions:
1. Season pork cutlets with salt and pepper, then dredge in flour.
2. Dip in beaten egg and coat with breadcrumbs.
3. Air fry at 190°C for 14 minutes, flipping halfway.

Air-Fried Pork and Cider Casserole

Serves 2 / Prep Time: 15 minutes / Cook Time: 30 minutes

Ingredients:
- 300g pork loin, cut into chunks
- 100g onion, finely chopped
- 1 carrot, sliced
- 1 celery stalk, chopped
- 10g garlic, minced
- 1 apple, peeled, cored, and diced
- 120ml apple cider
- 120ml chicken broth
- 1 tablespoon all-purpose flour
- 1 tablespoon vegetable oil
- 1 teaspoon dried thyme

- Salt and pepper, to taste
- Fresh parsley, for garnish (optional)

Instructions:

1. Preheat your air fryer to 375°F (190°C) for 5 minutes.
2. In a skillet, heat the vegetable oil over medium heat. Add the chopped onion, sliced carrot, chopped celery, and minced garlic. Sauté for 3-4 minutes until the vegetables begin to soften.
3. Add the pork loin chunks and cook until they start to brown.
4. Sprinkle the all-purpose flour over the mixture and stir for another minute to create a roux.
5. Pour in the apple cider and chicken broth while stirring continuously to create a flavorful sauce.
6. Stir in the diced apple and dried thyme. Season with salt and pepper.
7. Transfer the mixture to an ovenproof dish that fits into your air fryer.
8. Place the dish in the air fryer basket.
9. Air fry the pork and cider casserole for 25-30 minutes at 375°F (190°C) until the pork is cooked through, and the casserole is bubbling and slightly browned on top.
10. Optionally, garnish with fresh parsley before serving.

Air-Fried Beef and Broccoli

Serves 2 / Prep Time: 15 minutes / Cook Time: 15 minutes

Ingredients:

- 300g beef sirloin, thinly sliced
- 200g broccoli florets
- 60ml soy sauce
- 2 tablespoons brown sugar
- 2 cloves garlic, minced
- 1 tablespoon cornstarch
- 1 tablespoon vegetable oil
- Sesame seeds, for garnish (optional)

Instructions:

1. Preheat your air fryer to 375°F (190°C) for 5 minutes.
2. In a bowl, whisk together the soy sauce, brown sugar, minced garlic, and cornstarch until well combined. Set aside.
3. Season the thinly sliced beef with salt and

pepper.
4. Place the broccoli florets and seasoned beef in the air fryer basket.
5. Drizzle the vegetable oil over the Ingredients.
6. Air fry the beef and broccoli for 12-15 minutes at 375°F (190°C) until the beef is cooked through, and the broccoli is tender.
7. Pour the soy sauce mixture over the cooked beef and broccoli. Toss to coat.
8. Optionally, garnish with sesame seeds before serving.

Air-Fried Pork Schnitzel Sandwich

Serves 2 / Prep Time: 15 minutes / Cook Time: 10 minutes

Ingredients:

- 2 pork loin chops (150g each)
- 60g breadcrumbs
- 30g all-purpose flour
- 1 teaspoon paprika
- 1/2 teaspoon garlic powder
- 1/2 teaspoon onion powder
- 1 egg, beaten
- Salt and pepper, to taste
- 2 sandwich rolls
- Lettuce leaves
- Sliced tomatoes
- Dijon mustard or mayonnaise

Instructions:

1. In a bowl, mix the breadcrumbs, all-purpose flour, paprika, garlic powder, onion powder, salt, and pepper.
2. Dip each pork loin chop into the beaten egg and then coat them with the breadcrumb mixture.
3. Place the breaded pork chops in the air fryer basket.
4. Preheat your Ninja Foodi Dual Zone Air Fryer by selecting AIR FRY, setting the temperature to 375°F (190°C), and setting the time to 10 minutes. Select START/PAUSE to begin
5. Air fry for about 8-10 minutes, flipping halfway through, until the pork is golden brown and cooked through.
6. While the pork is cooking, slice the sandwich rolls and lightly toast them in the air fryer for 2-3 minutes.

7. Assemble your schnitzel sandwiches by placing lettuce leaves, sliced tomatoes, and the air-fried pork schnitzel on the toasted rolls.
8. Add Dijon mustard or mayonnaise as desired.
9. Serve hot.

Herb-Roasted Rack of Lamb

Serves 2 / Prep Time: 15 minutes / Cook Time: 20 minutes

Ingredients:
- 1 rack of lamb (400g)
- 2 tablespoons olive oil
- 2 cloves garlic, minced
- 1 teaspoon dried rosemary
- 1 teaspoon dried thyme
- Salt and pepper, to taste

Instructions:
1. In a bowl, mix the olive oil, minced garlic, dried rosemary, dried thyme, salt, and pepper.
2. Coat the rack of lamb with the herb mixture.
3. Place the rack of lamb in the air fryer basket, bone side down.
4. Preheat your Ninja Foodi Dual Zone Air Fryer by selecting AIR FRY, setting the temperature to 375°F (190°C), and setting the time to 20 minutes. Select START/PAUSE to begin
5. Air fry for about 18-20 minutes, or until the lamb reaches your desired level of doneness (medium-rare is recommended).
6. Rest the lamb for a few minutes before slicing and serving.

Air-Fried Lamb Kebabs with Tzatziki Sauce

Serves 2 / Prep Time: 20 minutes / Cook Time: 12 minutes

Ingredients:
- For the Lamb Kebabs:
- 300g ground lamb
- 25g breadcrumbs
- 30g finely chopped onion
- 2 cloves garlic, minced
- 1 teaspoon ground cumin
- 1 teaspoon ground coriander
- Salt and pepper, to taste
- Cooking spray or oil, for air frying
- For the Tzatziki Sauce:
- 120g Greek yogurt
- 100g cucumber, grated
- 1 clove garlic, minced
- 1 tablespoon fresh dill, chopped
- 1 tablespoon fresh lemon juice
- Salt and pepper, to taste

Instructions:
1. Preheat your air fryer to 375°F (190°C) for 5 minutes.
2. In a bowl, combine the ground lamb, breadcrumbs, chopped onion, minced garlic, ground cumin, ground coriander, salt, and pepper. Mix until well combined.
3. Form the mixture into 4 lamb kebabs.
4. Spray the air fryer basket with cooking spray or lightly oil it to prevent sticking.
5. Place the lamb kebabs in the air fryer basket.
6. Air fry the lamb kebabs for 10-12 minutes at 375°F (190°C) until they are cooked through and have a nice crust.
7. While the lamb kebabs are cooking, prepare the tzatziki sauce. In a bowl, combine the Greek yogurt, grated cucumber, minced garlic, chopped fresh dill, lemon juice, salt, and pepper. Mix until well combined.
8. Serve the lamb kebabs with the tzatziki sauce on the side.

Air-Fried Pork and Sage Meatloaf

Serves 2 / Prep Time: 15 minutes / Cook Time: 25 minutes

Ingredients:
- 300g ground pork
- 25g breadcrumbs
- 30g finely chopped onion
- 60ml milk
- 1 egg
- 1 tablespoon fresh sage, chopped
- 1/2 teaspoon dried thyme
- Salt and pepper, to taste
- Cooking spray or oil, for air frying

Instructions:
1. Preheat your air fryer to 375°F (190°C) for 5 minutes.

2. In a bowl, combine the ground pork, breadcrumbs, chopped onion, milk, egg, chopped fresh sage, dried thyme, salt, and pepper. Mix until well combined.
3. Form the mixture into a loaf shape.
4. Spray the air fryer basket with cooking spray or lightly oil it to prevent sticking.
5. Place the pork meatloaf in the air fryer basket.
6. Air fry the meatloaf for 20-25 minutes at 375°F (190°C) until it is cooked through and has a golden crust.
7. Let the meatloaf rest for a few minutes before slicing.

Jamaican Beef Patty

Serves: 4 / Prep Time: 30 minutes / Cook time: 20 minutes

Ingredients:
* For the pastry:
* 250g all-purpose flour
* 1/2 tsp turmeric powder (optional, for colour)
* 1/2 tsp salt
* 115g unsalted butter, cold and cubed
* 60ml ice water
* For the filling:
* 300g ground beef
* 1 small onion, finely chopped
* 1 clove garlic, minced
* 1 small carrot, finely grated
* 1 small potato, finely grated
* 2 tbsp vegetable oil
* 1 tsp curry powder
* 1/2 tsp dried thyme
* 1/4 tsp ground allspice
* Salt and black pepper, to taste
* 60ml beef or vegetable broth

Instructions:
1. Preheat the Ninja Dual Zone Air Fryer to 180°C on zone 1 for 5 minutes.
2. In a large bowl, combine the all-purpose flour, turmeric powder (if using), and salt for the pastry.
3. Add the cold cubed butter to the flour mixture and use your fingers or a pastry cutter to cut the butter into the flour until it resembles coarse crumbs.
4. Gradually add the ice water, a few tablespoons at a time, and mix until the dough comes together. Be careful not to overmix.
5. Shape the dough into a disk, wrap it in plastic wrap, and refrigerate for at least 15 minutes.
6. While the dough is chilling, prepare the filling. In a pan, heat the vegetable oil over medium heat.
7. Add the chopped onion and minced garlic to the pan and sauté for 2-3 minutes, until they are softened and aromatic.
8. Add the ground beef to the pan and cook until it is browned and cooked through.
9. Stir in the grated carrot, grated potato, curry powder, dried thyme, ground allspice, salt, black pepper, and beef or vegetable broth. Cook for an additional 5 minutes, or until the vegetables are tender and the flavours have melded together.
10. Remove the filling from the heat and let it cool slightly.

Jamaican Curry Goat

Serves: 4 / Prep Time: 20 minutes / Cook time: 1 hour 30 minutes

Ingredients:
* 800g goat meat, cut into bite-sized pieces
* 2 tbsp vegetable oil
* 1 onion, finely chopped
* 3 cloves garlic, minced
* 2 tsp Jamaican curry powder
* 1 tsp ground allspice
* 1 tsp dried thyme
* 1 scotch bonnet pepper, seeded and minced (optional)
* 2 potatoes, peeled and diced
* 2 carrots, peeled and sliced
* 400ml coconut milk
* 400ml chicken or vegetable broth
* Salt and black pepper, to taste
* Fresh cilantro, chopped (for garnish)

Instructions:
1. Preheat the Ninja Dual Zone Air Fryer to 180°C on zone 1 for 5 minutes.
2. In a large pan, heat the vegetable oil over medium heat. Add the chopped onion and minced garlic, and sauté until they are softened and fragrant.

3. Add the goat meat to the pan and brown it on all sides.
4. Sprinkle the Jamaican curry powder, ground allspice, dried thyme, and minced scotch bonnet pepper (if using) over the meat. Stir well to coat the meat with the spices.
5. Add the diced potatoes and sliced carrots to the pan, and pour in the coconut milk and chicken or vegetable broth.
6. Season with salt and black pepper to taste. Bring the mixture to a boil, then reduce the heat to low and simmer for 1 hour 30 minutes, or until the goat meat is tender and the flavours have melded together.
7. Once the curry goat is cooked, remove it from the heat and let it cool slightly.
8. Place the curry goat in a baking dish and place the dish in zone 1 of the air fryer. Cook at 180°C for 10 minutes to further enhance the flavours and thicken the sauce.
9. Once cooked, remove the curry goat from the air fryer and garnish with freshly chopped cilantro.

Steak and Kidney Pie

Serves: 4 / Prep Time: 20 minutes / Cook time: 1 hour

Ingredients:
- 500g diced beef steak
- 200g beef kidney, trimmed and diced
- 1 large onion, chopped
- 2 cloves garlic, minced
- 2 tbsp vegetable oil
- 2 tbsp all-purpose flour
- 300ml beef stock
- 2 tbsp Worcestershire sauce
- Salt and black pepper, to taste
- 1 sheet ready-made puff pastry
- 1 egg, beaten

Instructions:
1. Preheat the Ninja Dual Zone Air Fryer to 200°C on zone 1 for 5 minutes.
2. In a large frying pan, heat the oil over medium-high heat. Add the diced beef steak and beef kidney and cook until browned on all sides.
3. Add the chopped onion and minced garlic to the pan and cook until softened.

4. Sprinkle the flour over the meat and vegetables and stir to coat.
5. Gradually add the beef stock, stirring constantly until the mixture thickens.
6. Stir in the Worcestershire sauce and season with salt and black pepper to taste.
7. Transfer the mixture to a 20cm pie dish.
8. Roll out the puff pastry and cover the top of the pie dish, trimming any excess pastry.
9. Brush the beaten egg over the pastry to glaze.
10. Place the pie dish on the crisper plate in zone 1 and air fry at 200°C for 30-40 minutes or until the pastry is golden and crispy.

Roast Pork with Crackling

Serves: 4-6 / Prep Time: 10 minutes / Cook time: 50 minutes

Ingredients:
1. 5kg boneless pork loin
- 1 tbsp olive oil
- 1 tbsp sea salt
- 1 tbsp fennel seeds
- 2 garlic cloves, minced
- 2 sprigs of fresh rosemary
- 1 lemon, halved

Instructions:
1. Preheat the Ninja Dual Zone Air Fryer to 180°C on zone 1 for 5 minutes.
2. In a bowl, mix together the olive oil, sea salt, fennel seeds, minced garlic, and the leaves from one sprig of rosemary.
3. Rub the mixture all over the pork loin.
4. Place the pork loin on the crisper plate in zone 2 and air fry using the Roast function at 180°C for 40-50 minutes or until the internal temperature reaches 63°C.
5. Remove the pork loin from the air fryer and let it rest for 10 minutes.
6. While the pork is resting, use the Broil function on zone 1 to crisp up the crackling. Place the pork on the crisper plate, skin-side up, and broil for 5-10 minutes or until the crackling is crispy.
7. Once the crackling is done, remove the pork from the air fryer and place it on a cutting board.
8. Squeeze the lemon over the pork and sprinkle with the remaining rosemary leaves.

Chapter 5 Fish and seafood

South African Piri Piri Prawns

Prep Time: 25 minutes (including marination)
Cooking Time: 8 minutes / Servings: 2

Ingredients:
* 200g large prawns, peeled and deveined
* 2 tbsp piri piri sauce (store-bought or homemade)
* 1 tbsp lemon juice
* 2 garlic cloves, minced
* 1 tbsp olive oil
* Fresh parsley, chopped for garnish

Instructions:
1. Mix piri piri sauce, lemon juice, garlic, and olive oil in a bowl.
2. Toss prawns in the mixture and let marinate for 15 minutes.
3. Preheat the air fryer to 190°C.
4. Cook the prawns in the air fryer for 6-8 minutes or until pink and cooked through.
5. Garnish with fresh parsley before serving.

Turkish Spiced Mackerel with Yogurt Sauce

Prep Time: 10 minutes / Cooking Time: 10 minutes / Servings: 2

Ingredients:
* 2 mackerel fillets
* 2 tsp sumac
* 1 tsp smoked paprika
* 1 tsp cumin
* Salt and pepper to taste
* Olive oil for brushing
* Yoghourt Sauce:
* 150ml plain yoghourt
* 1 garlic clove, minced
* 1 tbsp fresh dill, chopped
* 1 tbsp lemon juice

Instructions:
1. Mix sumac, smoked paprika, cumin, salt, and pepper in a bowl.
2. Rub the spice mixture onto the mackerel fillets.
3. Preheat the air fryer to 190°C.

4. Brush the mackerel with olive oil and cook in the air fryer for 8-10 minutes.
5. For the yoghurt sauce, combine all Ingredients in a bowl.
6. Serve mackerel with a side of yoghurt sauce.

Spanish Garlic Shrimp Tapas (Gambas al Ajillo)

Prep Time: 10 minutes / Cooking Time: 8 minutes / Servings: 2

Ingredients:
* 200g large shrimp, peeled and deveined
* 50ml olive oil
* 5 garlic cloves, thinly sliced
* 1 tsp red chilli flakes
* 2 tbsp fresh parsley, chopped
* Salt to taste
* Lemon wedges for serving

Instructions:
1. In a bowl, mix olive oil, garlic, chilli flakes, parsley, and salt.
2. Toss shrimp in the mixture.
3. Preheat the air fryer to 190°C.
4. Cook the shrimp in the air fryer for 6-8 minutes or until pink and cooked through.
5. Serve immediately with lemon wedges.

Caribbean Coconut Lime Scallops

Prep Time: 25 minutes (including marination)
Cooking Time: 8 minutes / Servings: 2

Ingredients:
* 200g scallops
* 100ml coconut milk
* Zest and juice of 1 lime
* 1 tbsp fresh cilantro, chopped
* Salt and pepper to taste

Instructions:
1. In a bowl, mix coconut milk, lime zest, lime juice, cilantro, salt, and pepper.
2. Marinate scallops in the mixture for 15 minutes.
3. Preheat the air fryer to 190°C.

4. Cook the scallops in the air fryer for 6-8 minutes or until opaque and slightly golden.
5. Drizzle with any remaining marinade before serving.

Egyptian Spiced Tilapia with Tahini Drizzle

Prep Time: 10 minutes / Cooking Time: 10 minutes / Servings: 2

Ingredients:
* 2 tilapia fillets
* 2 tsp ground coriander
* 1 tsp ground cumin
* 1 tsp paprika
* Salt and pepper to taste
* Olive oil for brushing
* Tahini Drizzle:
* 50ml tahini
* 1 garlic clove, minced
* 2 tbsp lemon juice
* Water to thin, if needed

Instructions:
1. Mix coriander, cumin, paprika, salt, and pepper in a bowl.
2. Rub the spice mixture onto the tilapia fillets.
3. Preheat the air fryer to 190°C.
4. Brush the tilapia with olive oil and cook in the air fryer for 8-10 minutes.
5. For the tahini drizzle, whisk together tahini, garlic, and lemon juice. If too thick, add a little water.
6. Serve the tilapia with a generous drizzle of the tahini sauce.

New Zealand Green-Lipped Mussel Fritters

Prep Time: 15 minutes / Cooking Time: 10 minutes / Servings: 2-3

Ingredients:
* 250g green-lipped mussels, removed from shell and chopped
* 2 eggs
* 50g flour
* 1 red onion, finely chopped
* 2 tbsp fresh parsley, chopped
* Salt and pepper to taste
* Olive oil for brushing

Instructions:
1. In a bowl, mix mussels, eggs, flour, red onion, parsley, salt, and pepper until well combined.
2. Shape the mixture into small patties.
3. Preheat the air fryer to 190°C.
4. Brush the patties with olive oil and cook in the air fryer for 8-10 minutes or until golden brown.
5. Serve hot with lemon wedges.

Malaysian Sambal Stingray Packets

Prep Time: 15 minutes / Cooking Time: 15 minutes / Servings: 2

Ingredients:
* 2 stingray fillets (or skate wing fillets as an alternative)
* 3 tbsp sambal oelek (store-bought or homemade)
* 2 garlic cloves, minced
* 1 tbsp tamarind paste
* 1 tbsp sugar
* Banana leaves for wrapping (or aluminium foil)

Instructions:
1. Mix sambal oelek, garlic, tamarind paste, and sugar in a bowl.
2. Coat the stingray fillets with the sambal mixture.
3. Wrap each fillet in banana leaves or aluminium foil, sealing the edges.
4. Preheat the air fryer to 190°C.
5. Cook the wrapped stingray in the air fryer for 12-15 minutes.
6. Unwrap and serve immediately.

Canadian Maple-Glazed Salmon Bites

Prep Time: 25 minutes (including marination) Cooking Time: 10 minutes / Servings: 2-3

Ingredients:
* 300g salmon fillet, cut into bite-sized cubes
* 3 tbsp maple syrup
* 1 tbsp Dijon mustard
* 1 tbsp soy sauce
* Salt and pepper to taste

Instructions:
1. In a bowl, mix maple syrup, Dijon mustard, soy sauce, salt, and pepper.

2. Toss the salmon cubes in the marinade and let sit for 15 minutes.
3. Preheat the air fryer to 190°C.
4. Arrange the salmon bites in the air fryer and cook for 8-10 minutes until golden and slightly caramelised.
5. Serve immediately.

Portuguese Clams in Garlic and White Wine

Prep Time: 10 minutes / Cooking Time: 10 minutes / Servings: 2

Ingredients:
* 500g fresh clams, cleaned
* 100ml white wine
* 3 garlic cloves, minced
* 2 tbsp olive oil
* 2 tbsp fresh parsley, chopped
* 1 lemon, zest and juice
* Salt and pepper to taste

Instructions:
1. In a bowl, mix white wine, garlic, olive oil, parsley, lemon zest, lemon juice, salt, and pepper.
2. Toss the clams in the mixture.
3. Transfer the clams to a suitable air fryer dish.
4. Cook in the air fryer at 190°C for 8-10 minutes or until clams open up.
5. Serve with crusty bread to soak up the flavorful juices.

West African Spicy Prawn Kebabs

Prep Time: 15 minutes / Cooking Time: 8 minutes / Servings: 2

Ingredients:
* 200g large prawns, peeled and deveined
* 2 tbsp harissa paste
* 1 tbsp peanut oil
* 1 tsp smoked paprika
* 1 tsp ground ginger
* Salt to taste
* Wooden skewers, soaked in water

Instructions:
1. In a bowl, mix harissa, peanut oil, smoked paprika, ground ginger, and salt.

2. Toss prawns in the spice mixture.
3. Thread prawns onto soaked wooden skewers.
4. Preheat the air fryer to 190°C.
5. Cook the prawn kebabs in the air fryer for 6-8 minutes, turning halfway, until charred and cooked through.
6. Serve immediately with lime wedges.

Chilean Sea Bass with Pebre Sauce

Prep Time: 15 minutes / Cooking Time: 12 minutes / Servings: 2

Ingredients:
* 2 Chilean sea bass fillets
* 2 tbsp olive oil
* Salt and pepper to taste
* Pebre Sauce:
* 1 tomato, finely chopped
* 1 onion, finely chopped
* 2 garlic cloves, minced
* 2 green chilies, minced
* 3 tbsp fresh cilantro, chopped
* 2 tbsp red wine vinegar
* 1 tbsp olive oil
* Salt to taste

Instructions:
1. For the Pebre sauce, combine all Ingredients in a bowl and set aside to let flavours meld.
2. Brush the sea bass fillets with olive oil and season with salt and pepper.
3. Preheat the air fryer to 190°C.
4. Cook the sea bass in the air fryer for 10-12 minutes until flaky and golden.
5. Serve the sea bass with a generous spoonful of Pebre sauce

Korean Spicy Octopus Stir-fry (Nakji Bokkeum) Bites

Prep Time: 15 minutes / Cooking Time: 10 minutes / Servings: 2

Ingredients:
* 250g baby octopus, cleaned and cut into bite-sized pieces
* 2 tbsp gochujang (Korean red chilli paste)
* 1 tbsp soy sauce
* 1 tbsp honey

- 1 tsp sesame oil
- 2 garlic cloves, minced
- 1 green onion, chopped
- 1 tsp toasted sesame seeds

Instructions:
1. In a bowl, mix gochujang, soy sauce, honey, sesame oil, and garlic to create a marinade.
2. Toss the octopus pieces in the marinade.
3. Preheat the air fryer to 190°C.
4. Cook the octopus bites in the air fryer for 8-10 minutes, stirring halfway through.
5. Garnish with green onions and toasted sesame seeds.

Scottish Smoked Haddock Fishcakes with Tartar Sauce

Prep Time: 20 minutes / Cooking Time: 12 minutes / Servings: 2-3

Ingredients:
- 200g smoked haddock
- 100g mashed potatoes
- 2 tbsp fresh parsley, chopped
- 1 egg, beaten
- 100g breadcrumbs
- Olive oil for brushing
- Tartar Sauce:
- 100ml mayonnaise
- 1 tbsp capers, chopped
- 1 tbsp pickles, chopped
- 1 tsp lemon juice

Instructions:
1. Flake the smoked haddock and mix with mashed potatoes and parsley.
2. Shape the mixture into patties and dip each into the beaten egg, followed by breadcrumbs.
3. Preheat the air fryer to 190°C.
4. Brush the fishcakes with olive oil and cook in the air fryer for 10-12 minutes until golden and crispy.
5. For the tartar sauce, mix all Ingredients in a bowl.
6. Serve the fishcakes with a side of tartar sauce.

Air-Fried Baked Stuffed Clams

Serves 2 / Prep Time: 20 minutes / Cook Time: 10 minutes

Ingredients:
- 6 fresh clams in shells, scrubbed and cleaned
- 50g breadcrumbs
- 30g grated Parmesan cheese
- 2 cloves garlic, minced (10g)
- 2 tablespoons fresh parsley, chopped (10g)
- 2 tablespoons butter (30g), melted
- Salt and pepper, to taste
- Lemon wedges, for garnish (optional)

Instructions:
1. Preheat your air fryer to 375°F (190°C) for 5 minutes.
2. In a bowl, combine the breadcrumbs, grated Parmesan cheese, minced garlic, chopped parsley, melted butter, salt, and pepper.
3. Carefully open the clams and detach the meat from the shells. Place the clam meat on a plate. Spoon the breadcrumb mixture onto each clam meat, creating a stuffing.
4. Return the stuffed clam meat to the shells.
5. Place the stuffed clams in the air fryer basket.
6. Air fry the stuffed clams for 8-10 minutes at 375°F (190°C) until they are golden brown and the clams are cooked through.
7. Serve with lemon wedges, if desired.

Air-Fried Fisherman's Pie

Serves 2 / Prep Time: 20 minutes / Cook Time: 15 minutes

Ingredients:
- For the Filling:
- 200g white fish fillets, cut into chunks
- 100g cooked and peeled prawns
- 1 small onion, finely chopped (100g)
- 1 carrot, finely chopped (100g)
- 1/2 cup frozen peas (60g)
- 1 tablespoon olive oil (15g)
- 1 tablespoon all-purpose flour (10g)
- 1/2 cup fish or vegetable broth (120ml)
- 2 tablespoons heavy cream (30g)
- Salt and pepper, to taste
- For the Mashed Potato Topping:
- 2 large potatoes (300g), peeled and cut into chunks
- 2 tablespoons butter (30g)
- 2 tablespoons milk (30ml)

- Salt and pepper, to taste

Instructions:

1. Preheat your air fryer to 375°F (190°C) for 5 minutes.
2. In a skillet, heat the olive oil over medium heat. Add the chopped onion and carrot. Sauté for 2-3 minutes until they begin to soften.
3. Add the chunks of white fish fillets and cook until they start to turn opaque.
4. Sprinkle the all-purpose flour over the mixture and stir for another minute to create a roux.
5. Gradually pour in the fish or vegetable broth while stirring continuously to create a thick sauce.
6. Stir in the heavy cream and add the cooked and peeled prawns and frozen peas. Season with salt and pepper. Cook for an additional 2 minutes.
7. Transfer the fish and vegetable mixture to two individual ovenproof dishes.
8. In a separate pot, boil the peeled and chopped potatoes until they are tender. Drain and mash them with butter, milk, salt, and pepper until smooth.
9. Spoon the mashed potato topping over the fish and vegetable mixture in the ovenproof dishes.
10. Place the dishes in the air fryer basket.
11. Air fry the fisherman's pie for 12-15 minutes at 375°F (190°C) until the top is golden brown and the filling is bubbling.

Garlic Butter Shrimp

Serves 2 / Prep Time: 15 minutes / Cook Time: 8 minutes

Ingredients:

- 300g large shrimp, peeled and deveined
- 2 tablespoons unsalted butter, melted
- 4 cloves garlic, minced
- 1 tablespoon fresh parsley, chopped
- Salt and pepper, to taste
- Lemon wedges for garnish

Instructions:

1. Preheat the unit In a bowl, mix the melted butter, minced garlic, chopped parsley, salt, and pepper.
2. Toss the shrimp in the garlic butter mixture until coated.

3. Place the shrimp in the air fryer basket in a single layer.
4. Preheat your Ninja Foodi Air Fryer AF101 by selecting AIR FRY, setting the temperature to 375°F (190°C), and setting the time to 3 minutes. Select START/PAUSE to begin.
5. Air fry for about 6-8 minutes, until the shrimp are pink and opaque.
6. Serve with lemon wedges for garnish.

Lemon-Herb Grilled Salmon

Serves 2 / Prep Time: 10 minutes / Cook Time: 10 minutes

Ingredients:

- 2 salmon fillets (150g each)
- 2 tablespoons olive oil
- Zest and juice of 1 lemon
- 1 teaspoon dried dill
- 1 teaspoon dried thyme
- Salt and pepper, to taste
- Lemon wedges for garnish

Instructions:

1. Preheat your Ninja Foodi Air Fryer AF101 to 375°F (190°C).
2. In a bowl, mix the olive oil, lemon zest, lemon juice, dried dill, dried thyme, salt, and pepper.
3. Coat the salmon fillets with the lemon-herb mixture.
4. Place the salmon fillets in the air fryer basket.
5. Air fry for about 8-10 minutes, until the salmon flakes easily with a fork.
6. Serve with lemon wedges for garnish.

Smoked Mackerel Pâté

Serves 2 / Prep Time: 10 minutes / Cook Time: 0 minutes

Ingredients:

- 200g mackerel fillets
- 2 tablespoons cream cheese
- 1 tablespoon horseradish sauce
- Juice of 1/2 lemon
- Salt and pepper, to taste
- Fresh dill, for garnish

Instructions:

1. Begin by preheating your Air Fryer to 350 F.
2. Season the mackerel fillets with salt and place

in the Air Fryer.

3. Use the roast cooking preset and roast the fillet till they're crispy on the outside and moist on the inside. Feel free to Air fry is there's no roast option on your air fryer.
4. Begin by flaking the roasted mackerel fillets into a food processor.
5. Add in the cream cheese, horseradish sauce, and lemon juice to the food processor.
6. Season the mixture with salt and pepper.
7. Blend everything together until you achieve a smooth and creamy consistency.
8. Taste the pâté and adjust the seasoning, if necessary.
9. Transfer the roasted mackerel pâté to a bowl, cover, and refrigerate for at least 30 minutes before serving.
10. If desired, garnish with fresh dill before serving.

Air-Fried Cod with Tartar Sauce

Serves 2 / Prep Time: 10 minutes / Cook Time: 12 minutes

Ingredients:
* For the Cod:
* 2 cod fillets (200g each)
* 2 tablespoons olive oil
* Salt and pepper, to taste
* For the Tartar Sauce:
* 4 tablespoons mayonnaise
* 1 tablespoon pickles, finely chopped
* 1 teaspoon capers, chopped
* 1 teaspoon Dijon mustard
* 1/2 teaspoon lemon juice
* Salt and pepper, to taste

Instructions:
1. Preheat your air fryer to 375°F (190°C) for 5 minutes.
2. Season the cod fillets with salt and pepper and brush them with olive oil.
3. Place the cod fillets in the air fryer basket.
4. Air fry the cod fillets for 10-12 minutes at 375°F (190°C) until they are cooked through and have a crispy exterior.
5. While the cod is cooking, prepare the tartar sauce. In a small bowl, mix together the mayonnaise, chopped pickles, capers, Dijon

mustard, lemon juice, salt, and pepper.
6. Serve the air-fried cod with the homemade tartar sauce on the side.

Baja Fish Tacos with Cilantro Lime Sauce

Servings: 2 / Prep Time: 5 minutes / Cook Time: 6 minutes

Ingredients:
* For The Fish Tacos:
* 400 grams white fish fillets (such as cod or tilapia)
* 60 grams all-purpose flour
* 5 grams chili powder
* 2 grams garlic powder
* 2 grams cumin
* 2 grams paprika
* 2 grams salt
* 2 grams black pepper
* Vegetable oil (for frying)
* Corn tortillas
* Shredded cabbage or lettuce
* Sliced tomatoes
* Sliced red onions
* Fresh cilantro leaves (for garnish)
* For The Cilantro Lime Sauce:
* 120 ml mayonnaise
* 30 ml lime juice
* 15 grams fresh cilantro, chopped
* 1 clove garlic, minced
* Salt and pepper to taste

Instructions:
1. In a bowl, combine the flour, chili powder, garlic powder, cumin, paprika, salt, and black pepper to make the seasoning mixture for the fish.
2. Pat the fish fillets dry with paper towels and cut them into small strips.
3. Dip each fish strip into the seasoning mixture, coating all sides evenly.
4. Preheat your Ninja Dual Zone Air Fryer to 2000C
5. Carefully place the seasoned fish strips in the preheated Air Fryer and air fry them for 2-3 minutes per side, or until golden brown and crispy.
6. Remove the fried fish from your Ninja Dual

Zone Air Fryer and place them on a paper towel-lined plate.

7. To prepare the cilantro lime sauce, combine mayonnaise, lime juice, chopped cilantro, minced garlic, salt, and pepper in a bowl. Mix well until smooth and creamy.

8. Set your Ninja Dual Zone Air Fryer to "Reheat" and warm the corn tortillas in the air fryer for 2-3 minutes or until they are soft and pliable.

9. Assemble the Baja fish tacos by placing some shredded cabbage or lettuce on each tortilla, followed by the crispy fish strips.

10. Top with sliced tomatoes, sliced red onions, and fresh cilantro.

Honey Mustard Glazed Salmon

Servings: 2 / Prep Time: 30 minutes / Cook Time: 20 minutes

Ingredients:
* 300 grams salmon fillets
* 45 ml Dijon mustard
* 30 ml honey
* 15 ml soy sauce
* 15 ml lemon juice
* Garlic, minced
* Fresh dill, chopped
* Salt
* Black pepper

Instructions:
1. Preheat your Air Fryer to 200°C.
2. Whisk together the Dijon mustard, honey, soy sauce, lemon juice, minced garlic, chopped dill, salt, and black pepper to create the honey mustard glaze.
3. Place the salmon fillets in an oven-resistant dish and brush them generously with the honey mustard glaze, ensuring they are evenly coated.
4. Reserve a small amount of the glaze for later use.
5. Let the salmon marinate in the refrigerator for 15-30 minutes to allow the flavors to develop.
6. Once marinated, transfer the baking dish to your preheated Air Fryer and bake for about 12-15 minutes, or until the salmon is cooked through and flakes easily with a fork.

7. While baking, you can brush the salmon with the reserved honey mustard glaze a few times to add extra flavor and glaze.

8. Once cooked, remove the honey mustard glazed salmon from the oven and let it rest for a few minutes.

9. Serve the salmon hot with your favorite sides, such as roasted vegetables.

Sesame-Crusted Ahi Tuna

Serves: 2 / Prep Time: 10 minutes / Cook time: 8 minutes

Ingredients:
* 2 (150g each) ahi tuna steaks
* 2 tbsp sesame seeds
* 1/4 tsp salt
* 1/4 tsp black pepper
* 1/4 tsp garlic powder
* 1/4 tsp onion powder
* 1/4 tsp paprika
* 1/4 tsp cayenne pepper
* 1 tbsp olive oil

Instructions:
1. Preheat the Ninja Dual Zone Air Fryer to 200°C on the "BROIL" function.
2. In a shallow dish, mix together sesame seeds, salt, black pepper, garlic powder, onion powder, paprika, and cayenne pepper.
3. Brush the tuna steaks with olive oil, and then coat them evenly with the sesame seed mixture.
4. Place the coated tuna steaks on the crisper plate in Zone 1 of the air fryer.
5. Broil the tuna steaks for 4 minutes, then flip them over and broil for an additional 4 minutes.
6. Serve the sesame-crusted ahi tuna steaks with your favourite side dish.

Spicy Cajun Catfish

Serves: 2 / Prep Time: 10 minutes / Cook time: 12 minutes

Ingredients:
* 2 (170g each) catfish fillets
* 60g all-purpose flour
* 60g yellow cornmeal
* 1/2 tsp paprika

- 1/2 tsp garlic powder
- 1/2 tsp onion powder
- 1/2 tsp dried oregano
- 1/2 tsp dried thyme
- 1/2 tsp cayenne pepper
- 1/4 tsp salt
- 1/4 tsp black pepper
- 1 small egg, beaten
- 1 tbsp olive oil

Instructions:
1. Pat the catfish fillets dry with a paper towel.
2. In a shallow dish, mix together flour, cornmeal, paprika, garlic powder, onion powder, oregano, thyme, cayenne pepper, salt, and black pepper.
3. Dip each catfish fillet into the beaten egg, and then coat both sides with the flour mixture.
4. Brush the crisper plate with olive oil, and then place the coated catfish fillets on it in Zone 1 of the air fryer.
5. Roast the catfish fillets on "ROAST" function at 200°C for 6 minutes.
6. Flip the catfish fillets over and continue roasting for an additional 6 minutes.
7. Serve the spicy cajun catfish fillets with your favourite side dish.

Japanese Miso-Glazed Cod Fillets

Serves: 4
Prep Time: 10 minutes / Cook time: 10 minutes

Ingredients:
- 4 cod fillets (about 150g each)
- 2 tbsp white miso paste
- 2 tbsp sake
- 1 tbsp mirin
- 1 tbsp sugar
- 1 tbsp vegetable oil
- 1 tbsp sesame seeds
- 2 green onions, thinly sliced
- Lime wedges, for serving

Instructions:
1. Preheat the Ninja Dual Zone Air Fryer to 200°C on zone 1 for 5 minutes.
2. In a small bowl, whisk together the miso paste, sake, mirin, and sugar until smooth.
3. Brush the cod fillets with the miso mixture, making sure to coat both sides evenly.
4. Place the fillets on the crisper plate in zone 1 and air fry at 200°C for 10 minutes, or until the fish is cooked through and the glaze is caramelised.
5. While the fish is cooking, heat the vegetable oil in a small skillet over medium heat. Add the sesame seeds and cook, stirring frequently, until lightly toasted.
6. Remove the fish from the air fryer and sprinkle with the toasted sesame seeds and sliced green onions. Serve with lime wedges.

Mexican Chipotle Lime Grilled Shrimp

Serves: 4
Prep Time: 15 minutes / Cook time: 5 minutes

Ingredients:
- 1 kg large shrimp, peeled and deveined
- 2 tbsp olive oil
- 2 tbsp adobo sauce (from a can of chipotle peppers in adobo sauce)
- Juice of 1 lime
- 1 tsp garlic powder
- 1 tsp onion powder
- Salt and pepper, to taste
- Chopped fresh cilantro, for serving

Instructions:
1. Preheat the Ninja Dual Zone Air Fryer to 200°C on zone 1 for 5 minutes.
2. In a large bowl, whisk together the olive oil, adobo sauce, lime juice, garlic powder, onion powder, salt, and pepper.
3. Add the shrimp to the bowl and toss to coat evenly with the marinade.
4. Place the shrimp on the crisper plate in zone 1 and air fry at 200°C for 5 minutes, or until the shrimp are cooked through and lightly charred.
5. Remove the shrimp from the air fryer and sprinkle with chopped cilantro. Serve immediately.

Chapter 6 Vegetable and Vegetarian

Air Fryer Thai Vegan Pineapple Fried Rice

Prep Time: 20 minutes / Cooking Time: 25 minutes / Servings: 4

Ingredients:
* 200g rice, cooked
* 1 small pineapple, hollowed out and diced
* 1 red bell pepper, diced
* 1 carrot, diced
* 100g cashews
* 2 tbsp soy sauce
* 1 tbsp coconut oil
* 2 spring onions, sliced
* 1 tsp curry powder
* Salt to taste

Instructions:
1. In a pan, heat coconut oil and sauté bell pepper and carrot until softened.
2. Add cooked rice, pineapple, cashews, soy sauce, curry powder, and salt. Mix well.
3. Transfer the mixture to the hollowed-out pineapple shell.
4. Air fry at 180°C for 25 minutes.
5. Garnish with sliced spring onions before serving.

Air Fryer Polish Vegan Pierogi

Prep Time: 45 minutes / Cooking Time: 20 minutes / Servings: 4

Ingredients:
* 200g all-purpose flour
* 100ml water
* 1 tbsp olive oil
* 200g mushrooms, finely chopped
* 100g sauerkraut, drained
* 1 onion, chopped
* 2 cloves garlic, minced
* Salt and pepper to taste

Instructions:
1. For the dough, mix flour, water, and a pinch of salt until a soft dough forms. Let it rest for 30 minutes.
2. In a pan, sauté onions and garlic in olive oil.

Add mushrooms and sauerkraut. Season with salt and pepper.
3. Roll out the dough thinly and cut out circles using a cookie cutter.
4. Place a spoonful of filling in the centre of each circle and fold over, pressing the edges to seal.
5. Air fry the pierogi at 180°C for 20 minutes or until golden.

Air Fryer Japanese Vegan Tempura

Prep Time: 20 minutes / Cooking Time: 15 minutes / Servings: 4

Ingredients:
* Assorted vegetables (bell peppers, zucchini, sweet potatoes), sliced
* 100g all-purpose flour
* 150ml cold sparkling water
* 1 tsp baking powder
* Salt to taste
* Soy sauce for dipping

Instructions:
1. In a bowl, whisk together flour, cold sparkling water, baking powder, and salt to form a smooth batter.
2. Dip vegetable slices into the batter, ensuring they are fully coated.
3. Air fry the coated vegetables at 200°C for 15 minutes or until golden and crispy.
4. Serve hot with soy sauce.

Air Fryer Mexican Vegan Tofu Tacos

Prep Time: 25 minutes / Cooking Time: 20 minutes / Servings: 4

Ingredients:
* 200g firm tofu, crumbled
* 2 tbsp olive oil
* 1 tsp smoked paprika
* 1 tsp ground cumin
* 1 tsp chilli powder
* 4 vegan taco shells
* Fresh lettuce, diced tomatoes, and avocado slices for serving

- Vegan sour cream and salsa

Instructions:

1. In a pan, heat olive oil and sauté crumbled tofu until slightly golden.
2. Add smoked paprika, cumin, and chilli powder. Cook for an additional 5 minutes.
3. Spoon the tofu mixture into taco shells.
4. Top with lettuce, tomatoes, avocado, vegan sour cream, and salsa.

Air Fryer French Vegan Ratatouille

Prep Time: 30 minutes / Cooking Time: 40 minutes / Servings: 4

Ingredients:

- 1 zucchini, sliced
- 1 eggplant, sliced
- 1 bell pepper, sliced
- 2 tomatoes, chopped
- 1 onion, chopped
- 3 cloves garlic, minced
- 2 tbsp olive oil
- 1 tsp dried thyme
- 1 tsp dried rosemary
- Salt and pepper to taste

Instructions:

1. In a pan, heat olive oil and sauté onions and garlic.
2. Add zucchini, eggplant, bell pepper, and tomatoes.
3. Season with thyme, rosemary, salt, and pepper.
4. Transfer the mixture to an air fryer-safe dish.
5. Air fry at 180°C for 40 minutes or until vegetables are tender and flavours melded.

Air Fryer German Vegan Potato Pancakes

Prep Time: 20 minutes / Cooking Time: 20 minutes / Servings: 4

Ingredients:

- 500g potatoes, peeled and grated
- 1 onion, grated
- 100g all-purpose flour
- 1 tsp baking powder
- Salt and pepper to taste
- Vegan apple sauce for serving

Instructions:

1. In a bowl, mix grated potatoes, onion, flour,

baking powder, salt, and pepper.

2. Shape the mixture into small patties.
3. Air fry the patties at 190°C for 20 minutes or until golden and crispy.
4. Serve hot with vegan applesauce.

Air Fryer Moroccan Vegan Chickpea Tagine

Prep Time: 20 minutes / Cooking Time: 30 minutes / Servings: 4

Ingredients:

- 400g chickpeas, cooked
- 2 carrots, chopped
- 1 zucchini, chopped
- 400g canned tomatoes, diced
- 1 onion, finely sliced
- 3 cloves garlic, minced
- 2 tbsp olive oil
- 1 tsp ground cumin
- 1 tsp ground coriander
- 1 tsp paprika
- Salt and pepper to taste
- Fresh coriander for garnish

Instructions:

1. In a pan, heat olive oil and sauté onions and garlic until translucent.
2. Add carrots, zucchini, spices, and cook for another 5 minutes.
3. Mix in chickpeas and tomatoes.
4. Transfer the mixture to an air fryer-safe dish.
5. Air fry at 170°C for 30 minutes.
6. Garnish with fresh coriander before serving.

Air Fryer Australian Vegan Damper Bread

Prep Time: 15 minutes / Cooking Time: 25 minutes / Servings: 4

Ingredients:

- 500g all-purpose flour
- 2 tsp baking powder
- 1 tsp salt
- 300ml cold water
- Olive oil for brushing

Instructions:

1. In a bowl, mix flour, baking powder, and salt.
2. Gradually add water, mixing until a soft dough

forms.

3. Shape into a round loaf and make a cross on the top with a sharp knife.
4. Brush with olive oil.
5. Air fry at 180°C for 25 minutes or until golden and sounds hollow when tapped.

Air Fryer Cuban Vegan Black Bean Bowl

Prep Time: 25 minutes / Cooking Time: 20 minutes / Servings: 4

Ingredients:
- 400g black beans, cooked
- 1 red bell pepper, sliced
- 1 green bell pepper, sliced
- 1 onion, sliced
- 2 tbsp olive oil
- Juice of 1 lime
- 1 tsp smoked paprika
- Salt and pepper to taste
- Fresh cilantro for garnish

Instructions:
1. In a bowl, toss bell peppers and onion in olive oil, paprika, salt, and pepper.
2. Air fry the vegetables at 190°C for 15 minutes or until slightly charred.
3. Mix roasted vegetables with black beans and lime juice.
4. Garnish with fresh cilantro before serving.

Air Fryer Kenyan Vegan Sukuma Wiki

Prep Time: 15 minutes / Cooking Time: 20 minutes / Servings: 4

Ingredients:
- 500g collard greens, chopped
- 1 onion, chopped
- 2 tomatoes, chopped
- 3 cloves garlic, minced
- 2 tbsp olive oil
- 1 tsp ground cumin
- Salt and pepper to taste

Instructions:
1. In a pan, heat olive oil and sauté onions and garlic until translucent.
2. Add tomatoes and cook until softened.

3. Mix in collard greens, ground cumin, salt, and pepper.
4. Transfer to an air fryer-safe dish.
5. Air fry at 180°C for 20 minutes.

Air Fryer Greek Vegan Spanakopita Bites

Prep Time: 30 minutes / Cooking Time: 20 minutes / Servings: 4

Ingredients:
- 400g fresh spinach, chopped
- 200g vegan feta cheese, crumbled
- 2 tbsp olive oil
- 1 onion, finely chopped
- 3 cloves garlic, minced
- 2 tsp dried dill
- 1 package vegan phyllo dough
- Salt and pepper to taste

Instructions:
1. In a pan, heat 1 tbsp olive oil and sauté onions and garlic until translucent.
2. Add spinach and cook until wilted. Season with salt, pepper, and dill.
3. Remove from heat and mix in crumbled vegan feta.
4. Cut phyllo dough into squares and brush with remaining olive oil.
5. Place a spoonful of spinach mixture in the centre of each square and fold into triangles.
6. Air fry the triangles at 190°C for 20 minutes or until golden and crispy.

Air Fryer Brazilian Vegan Coxinha

Prep Time: 40 minutes / Cooking Time: 25 minutes / Servings: 4

Ingredients:
- 200g canned young jackfruit, drained and shredded
- 100g vegan cream cheese
- 300g potatoes, boiled and mashed
- 1 onion, chopped
- 3 cloves garlic, minced
- 2 tbsp olive oil
- 1 tsp smoked paprika
- Salt and pepper to taste

- Vegan breadcrumbs for coating

Instructions:

1. In a pan, heat olive oil and sauté onions and garlic.
2. Add shredded jackfruit, smoked paprika, salt, and pepper. Cook until the jackfruit is tender.
3. Mix in vegan cream cheese and set aside to cool.
4. Shape mashed potatoes into small balls and flatten. Place a spoonful of jackfruit mixture in the centre and enclose the filling.
5. Roll the coxinhas in breadcrumbs.
6. Air fry at 190°C for 25 minutes or until golden brown.

Air Fryer Spanish Vegan Paella Bites

Prep Time: 30 minutes / Cooking Time: 25 minutes / Servings: 4

Ingredients:

- 200g Arborio rice, cooked
- 100g green peas
- 1 red bell pepper, diced
- 1 tomato, chopped
- 1 onion, chopped
- 2 cloves garlic, minced
- 1 tsp smoked paprika
- 1 tsp saffron threads
- 2 tbsp olive oil
- Salt and pepper to taste

Instructions:

1. In a pan, heat olive oil and sauté onions, garlic, and bell pepper.
2. Add tomato, green peas, smoked paprika, saffron, salt, and pepper. Cook for a few minutes.
3. Mix in cooked rice and stir well.
4. Shape the mixture into small balls.
5. Air fry at 190°C for 25 minutes or until crispy and golden.

Air Fryer Turkish Vegan Kofte

Prep Time: 30 minutes / Cooking Time: 20 minutes / Servings: 4

Ingredients:

- 400g tempeh, crumbled
- 1 onion, grated
- 2 cloves garlic, minced
- 2 tsp ground cumin
- 1 tsp ground coriander
- 1 tsp smoked paprika
- 2 tbsp fresh parsley, chopped
- 2 tbsp olive oil
- Salt and pepper to taste

Instructions:

1. In a bowl, combine crumbled tempeh, grated onion, garlic, spices, parsley, salt, and pepper. Mix well.
2. Shape the mixture into elongated meatballs.
3. Brush with olive oil.
4. Air fry at 190°C for 20 minutes or until golden and cooked through.

Air Fryer Italian Vegan Eggplant Parmesan

Prep Time: 30 minutes / Cooking Time: 25 minutes / Servings: 4

Ingredients:

- 2 medium eggplants, thinly sliced
- 400g canned tomatoes, crushed
- 2 cloves garlic, minced
- 200g vegan mozzarella cheese, grated
- 50g vegan parmesan cheese, grated
- 2 tbsp olive oil
- 1 tsp dried basil
- 1 tsp dried oregano
- Salt and pepper to taste

Instructions:

1. Brush eggplant slices with olive oil and season with salt and pepper.
2. Air fry at 190°C for 15 minutes or until golden brown.
3. In a pan, sauté garlic until fragrant. Add crushed tomatoes, basil, oregano, salt, and pepper. Simmer for 10 minutes.
4. In an air fryer-safe dish, layer fried eggplant slices, tomato sauce, and vegan cheeses. Repeat layers until all Ingredients are used.
5. Air fry at 180°C for 25 minutes or until bubbly and golden on top.

Air Fryer Thai Vegan Spring Rolls

Prep Time: 40 minutes / Cooking Time: 20 minutes / Servings: 4

Ingredients:

* 10 vegan spring roll wrappers
* 100g vermicelli noodles, cooked
* 50g shredded carrots
* 50g sliced bell peppers
* 50g thinly sliced cabbage
* 3 green onions, chopped
* 2 tbsp soy sauce
* 1 tbsp sesame oil
* Vegan sweet chilli sauce for dipping

Instructions:

1. In a bowl, mix vermicelli noodles, carrots, bell peppers, cabbage, and green onions. Toss with soy sauce and sesame oil.
2. Place a portion of the filling onto each spring roll wrapper and roll tightly.
3. Air fry at 190°C for 20 minutes or until crispy and golden.
4. Serve hot with vegan sweet chilli sauce.

Air Fryer Lebanese Vegan Falafel

Prep Time: 40 minutes (plus soaking time)
Cooking Time: 20 minutes / Servings: 4

Ingredients:

* 400g dried chickpeas, soaked overnight
* 1 onion, chopped
* 3 cloves garlic, minced
* 2 tsp ground cumin
* 1 tsp ground coriander
* 1 tsp chilli powder
* 2 tbsp fresh parsley, chopped
* 2 tbsp fresh cilantro, chopped
* Salt to taste

Instructions:

1. Drain and rinse soaked chickpeas. Blend with onion, garlic, spices, parsley, and cilantro until a coarse mixture forms.
2. Shape the mixture into small balls.
3. Air fry at 190°C for 20 minutes or until golden brown and crispy.
4. Serve with vegan tahini sauce or in a pita pocket with veggies.

Air Fryer Russian Vegan Borscht Bites

Prep Time: 30 minutes / Cooking Time: 25 minutes / Servings: 4

Ingredients:

* 2 medium beets, grated
* 1 carrot, grated
* 1 onion, finely chopped
* 2 cloves garlic, minced
* 2 tbsp olive oil
* 1 tsp dried dill
* Salt and pepper to taste
* Vegan sour cream for dipping

Instructions:

1. In a pan, heat olive oil and sauté onions and garlic until translucent.
2. Add grated beets and carrots, cooking until softened. Season with dill, salt, and pepper.
3. Let the mixture cool slightly, then shape into small patties.
4. Air fry at 190°C for 25 minutes or until crispy and cooked through.
5. Serve with vegan sour cream.

Air Fryer Japanese Vegan Okonomiyaki

Prep Time: 20 minutes / Cooking Time: 20 minutes / Servings: 4

Ingredients:

* 200g all-purpose flour
* 300ml vegetable broth
* 1 tbsp soy sauce
* 1 tsp baking powder
* 2 cups shredded cabbage
* 1 carrot, grated
* 2 green onions, chopped
* Vegan mayonnaise and seaweed flakes for garnish

Instructions:

1. In a bowl, mix flour, vegetable broth, soy sauce, and baking powder to form a batter.
2. Fold in cabbage, carrot, and green onions.
3. Scoop batter into the air fryer tray, forming pancakes.
4. Air fry at 190°C for 20 minutes, flipping halfway through.
5. Garnish with vegan mayo and seaweed flakes.

Air Fryer German Vegan Potato Pancakes

Prep Time: 20 minutes / Cooking Time: 25 minutes / Servings: 4

Ingredients:
- 500g potatoes, peeled and grated
- 1 onion, grated
- 50g all-purpose flour
- 1 tsp baking powder
- Salt and pepper to taste
- Apple sauce for serving

Instructions:
1. Squeeze out excess moisture from grated potatoes.
2. Mix potatoes, onion, flour, baking powder, salt, and pepper.
3. Shape into flat pancakes.
4. Air fry at 190°C for 25 minutes, flipping halfway through.
5. Serve hot with applesauce.

Air Fryer Mexican Vegan Tofu Tacos

Prep Time: 30 minutes / Cooking Time: 20 minutes / Servings: 4

Ingredients:
- 400g firm tofu, crumbled
- 2 tbsp olive oil
- 1 tsp ground cumin
- 1 tsp smoked paprika
- 1 tsp chilli powder
- 4 vegan tortillas
- Fresh salsa, lettuce, and vegan sour cream for serving

Instructions:
1. In a bowl, mix crumbled tofu with olive oil, cumin, paprika, and chilli powder.
2. Spread tofu mixture on the air fryer tray.
3. Air fry at 190°C for 20 minutes or until crispy.
4. Serve tofu on tortillas with salsa, lettuce, and vegan sour cream.

Air Fryer French Vegan Ratatouille Bites

Prep Time: 30 minutes / Cooking Time: 25 minutes / Servings: 4

Ingredients:
- 1 zucchini, diced
- 1 eggplant, diced
- 1 bell pepper, diced
- 1 tomato, diced
- 2 cloves garlic, minced
- 2 tbsp olive oil
- 1 tsp dried herbs de Provence
- Salt and pepper to taste

Instructions:
1. In a bowl, toss vegetables with olive oil, garlic, herbs, salt, and pepper.
2. Spread vegetable mixture on the air fryer tray.
3. Air fry at 190°C for 25 minutes or until vegetables are tender.
4. Serve hot as a side dish or snack.

Air Fryer British Vegan "Fish" and Chips

Prep Time: 40 minutes / Cooking Time: 25 minutes / Servings: 4

Ingredients:
- 400g firm tofu, sliced into "fillets"
- 500g potatoes, cut into chips
- 100g vegan breadcrumbs
- 2 tbsp olive oil
- 1 tsp seaweed flakes
- Salt and vinegar to taste

Instructions:
1. Brush tofu fillets with olive oil, then coat with breadcrumbs and seaweed flakes.
2. Spread tofu and potato chips on the air fryer tray, ensuring they don't overlap.
3. Air fry at 190°C for 25 minutes, flipping halfway through.
4. Serve hot with salt and vinegar.

Air Fryer Indian Vegan Samosas

Prep Time: 45 minutes / Cooking Time: 20 minutes / Servings: 4

Ingredients:
- 200g potatoes, boiled and mashed
- 100g green peas, boiled
- 1 onion, finely chopped
- 2 cloves garlic, minced
- 1 tsp ground cumin
- 1 tsp ground coriander
- 1 tsp garam masala
- 2 tbsp olive oil
- Vegan samosa wrappers

Instructions:

1. In a pan, heat oil and sauté onions and garlic until translucent.
2. Add spices and cook for a minute. Mix in mashed potatoes and peas.
3. Place a spoonful of filling in each samosa wrapper and fold into triangles.
4. Air fry at 190°C for 20 minutes or until golden brown.
5. Serve with vegan mint chutney.

Air Fryer Caribbean Vegan Jerk Jackfruit Sliders

Prep Time: 30 minutes / Cooking Time: 25 minutes / Servings: 4

Ingredients:

* 400g canned young jackfruit, drained and shredded
* 2 tbsp jerk seasoning
* 2 tbsp olive oil
* Vegan slider buns
* Vegan coleslaw for serving

Instructions:

1. Toss shredded jackfruit with olive oil and jerk seasoning.
2. Spread jackfruit on the air fryer tray.
3. Air fry at 190°C for 25 minutes or until crispy.
4. Serve on slider buns with coleslaw.

Air Fryer Australian Vegan "Sausage" Rolls

Prep Time: 40 minutes / Cooking Time: 25 minutes / Servings: 4

Ingredients:

* 200g mushrooms, finely chopped
* 100g walnuts, finely chopped
* 1 onion, finely chopped
* 2 cloves garlic, minced
* 1 tsp dried thyme
* 2 tbsp olive oil
* Vegan puff pastry

Instructions:

1. In a pan, heat oil and sauté onions and garlic until translucent.
2. Add mushrooms, walnuts, and thyme. Cook until mushrooms are tender.

3. Roll out puff pastry and cut into rectangles. Place a spoonful of filling on each rectangle and roll tightly.
4. Air fry at 190°C for 25 minutes or until golden brown.
5. Serve hot with vegan ketchup.

Air-Fried Veggie Spring Rolls

Serves 2 / Prep Time: 20 minutes / Cook Time: 10 minutes

Ingredients:

* 100g rice vermicelli noodles (cooked and drained)
* 8 spring roll wrappers
* 1 cup mixed vegetables (carrots, bell peppers, cabbage) - thinly sliced
* 1/2 cup fresh bean sprouts
* 1/4 cup fresh mint leaves
* 1/4 cup fresh cilantro leaves
* 1 tbsp soy sauce
* 1 tsp sesame oil
* 1 tsp rice vinegar
* 1/2 tsp sugar
* 1/4 tsp red pepper flakes
* Water (for sealing wrappers)

Instructions:

1. In a bowl, combine the cooked rice vermicelli noodles, mixed vegetables, bean sprouts, mint leaves, and cilantro leaves.
2. In a separate bowl, mix together the soy sauce, sesame oil, rice vinegar, sugar, and red pepper flakes. Pour this dressing over the noodle and vegetable mixture. Toss to combine.
3. Lay a spring roll wrapper flat on a clean surface. Place a small amount of the noodle and vegetable mixture near one edge of the wrapper.
4. Fold the sides of the wrapper in, then roll it up tightly, sealing the edges with a little water.
5. Preheat your air fryer to 200°C (390°F) for about 5 minutes.
6. Place the spring rolls in the air fryer basket without overcrowding. Air fry at 200°C (390°F) for about 10 minutes, turning them halfway through until they are golden brown and crispy.
7. Serve the veggie spring rolls hot, with dipping sauce of your choice.

Air-Fried Stuffed Mushrooms with Spinach and Vegan Chees

Serves 2 / Prep Time: 15 minutes / Cook Time: 10 minutes

Ingredients:

* 200g large mushrooms (cremini or white)
* 100g fresh spinach (chopped)
* 50g vegan cheese (shredded)
* 1 clove garlic (minced)
* 1/4 tsp red pepper flakes (optional)
* Salt and pepper to taste
* 1 tbsp olive oil

Instructions:

1. Remove the stems from the mushrooms and set them aside.
2. In a pan, heat olive oil over medium heat. Add minced garlic and sauté until fragrant.
3. Add chopped spinach to the pan and cook until wilted. Remove excess moisture if necessary.
4. In a bowl, combine the sautéed spinach, vegan cheese, red pepper flakes (if using), salt, and pepper.
5. Fill each mushroom cap with the spinach and cheese mixture.
6. Preheat your air fryer to 180°C (360°F) for about 5 minutes.
7. Place the stuffed mushrooms in the air fryer basket without overcrowding. Air fry at 180°C (360°F) for about 10 minutes until the mushrooms are tender and the cheese is melted.
8. Serve the stuffed mushrooms hot, and enjoy!

Chickpea Snack Mix

Serves 2 / Prep Time: 5 minutes / Cook Time: 10 minutes

Ingredients:

* 200g canned chickpeas, drained and rinsed
* 20g almonds
* 20g cashews
* 10g pumpkin seeds
* 10g sunflower seeds
* 1 tablespoon olive oil
* 1 teaspoon smoked paprika
* 1/2 teaspoon garlic powder
* 1/2 teaspoon cumin
* Salt and pepper, to taste

Instructions:

1. In a bowl, mix together the chickpeas, almonds, cashews, pumpkin seeds, sunflower seeds, olive oil, smoked paprika, garlic powder, cumin, salt, and pepper.
2. Preheat your Ninja Foodi Dual Zone Air Fryer to 375°F (190°C).
3. Place the mixture in the air fryer basket.
4. Select Zone 1, select AIRFRY, set temperature to 375°F (190°C), and set the time to 10 minutes.
5. Air fry for about 8-10 minutes, shaking the basket occasionally, until everything is crispy and golden.
6. Allow it to cool before serving as a tasty snack.

Crispy Air-Fried Eggplant Slices

Serves 2 / Prep Time: 10 minutes / Cook Time: 15 minutes

Ingredients:

* 1 medium eggplant, sliced into rounds
* 60g breadcrumbs
* 20g grated Parmesan cheese
* 1 teaspoon dried oregano
* 1/2 teaspoon garlic powder
* Salt and pepper, to taste
* Olive oil spray

Instructions:

1. Preheat your Ninja Foodi Dual Zone Air Fryer to 375°F (190°C).
2. In a bowl, mix together the breadcrumbs, grated Parmesan cheese, dried oregano, garlic powder, salt, and pepper.
3. Dip each eggplant slice into the breadcrumb mixture, pressing the mixture onto both sides.
4. Place the breaded eggplant slices in the air fryer basket.
5. Lightly spray the eggplant slices with olive oil.
6. Air fry for about 12-15 minutes, flipping once halfway through, until the slices are crispy and golden.
7. Serve the crispy air-fried eggplant slices as a side dish or snack.

Chapter 7 Sides and appetisers

Air Fryer Caribbean Vegan Sweet Potato Fritters

Prep Time: 30 minutes / Cooking Time: 20 minutes / Servings: 4

Ingredients:
- 300g sweet potatoes, boiled and mashed
- 1 chilli pepper, finely chopped
- 2 green onions, finely chopped
- 1 tsp ground allspice
- Salt to taste
- 50g breadcrumbs

Instructions:
1. Mix mashed sweet potatoes with chilli pepper, green onions, allspice, and salt.
2. Shape the mixture into small patties and coat with breadcrumbs.
3. Air fry at 190°C for 20 minutes or until crispy and golden.

Air Fryer Greek Vegan Spanakopita Triangles

Prep Time: 30 minutes / Cooking Time: 15 minutes / Servings: 4

Ingredients:
- Vegan phyllo dough sheets
- 200g fresh spinach, chopped
- 100g vegan feta, crumbled
- 1 onion, finely chopped
- 2 tbsp olive oil
- Salt and pepper to taste

Instructions:
1. In a pan, sauté onions in olive oil until translucent. Add spinach and cook until wilted. Season with salt and pepper.
2. Mix in crumbled vegan feta.
3. Cut phyllo sheets into strips and place a spoonful of the mixture at one end. Fold into triangles.
4. Air fry at 180°C for 15 minutes or until golden.

Air Fryer Brazilian Vegan Coxinha

Prep Time: 45 minutes / Cooking Time: 20 minutes / Servings: 4

Ingredients:
- 300g potatoes, boiled and mashed
- 200g young jackfruit, shredded and cooked
- 1 onion, chopped
- 2 cloves garlic, minced
- 2 tbsp vegan mayonnaise
- Salt and chilli powder to taste
- Breadcrumbs for coating

Instructions:
1. Sauté onion and garlic. Add jackfruit and season with salt and chili. Stir in vegan mayonnaise.
2. Take a portion of the mashed potatoes, flatten it, place the jackfruit mixture in the centre, and shape into a teardrop.
3. Coat with breadcrumbs.
4. Air fry at 190°C for 20 minutes or until golden.

Air Fryer Moroccan Vegan Stuffed Peppers

Prep Time: 20 minutes / Cooking Time: 25 minutes / Servings: 4

Ingredients:
- 4 bell peppers, tops removed and deseeded
- 200g couscous, cooked
- 50g raisins
- 2 tbsp olive oil
- 1 tsp cumin
- 1 tsp paprika
- Salt to taste

Instructions:
1. Mix cooked couscous with raisins, olive oil, cumin, paprika, and salt.
2. Stuff each bell pepper with the couscous mixture.
3. Air fry at 180°C for 25 minutes or until peppers are tender.

Air Fryer Vietnamese Vegan Spring Rolls

Prep Time: 30 minutes / Cooking Time: 15 minutes / Servings: 4

Ingredients:
* Vegan rice paper sheets
* 100g vermicelli noodles, cooked
* 1 carrot, julienned
* 1 cucumber, julienned
* Fresh mint and cilantro leaves
* Soy sauce for dipping

Instructions:
1. On a wet rice paper sheet, place a handful of vermicelli noodles, carrot, cucumber, and herbs.
2. Roll tightly, tucking in the sides.
3. Air fry at 180°C for 15 minutes or until crispy.
4. Serve with soy sauce.

Air Fryer Spanish Vegan Patatas Bravas

Prep Time: 15 minutes / Cooking Time: 20 minutes / Servings: 4

Ingredients:
* 300g potatoes, cubed
* 2 tbsp olive oil
* Salt and paprika to taste
* 100ml tomato sauce
* 1 tsp smoked paprika

Instructions:
1. Toss potato cubes with olive oil, salt, and paprika.
2. Air fry at 190°C for 20 minutes or until golden and crispy.
3. Mix tomato sauce with smoked paprika and heat.
4. Serve potatoes with the smoky tomato sauce.

Air Fryer Roasted Pickled Beets

Prep Time: 10 minutes / Cooking Time: 15 minutes / Servings: 4

Ingredients:
* 300g beets, peeled and sliced
* 250ml white vinegar
* 2 tbsp sugar
* 1 tsp salt
* 1 tsp black peppercorns

Instructions:
1. Air fry the beet slices at 180°C for 15 minutes or until slightly crispy.
2. In a jar, combine white vinegar, sugar, salt, and peppercorns. Stir until sugar dissolves.
3. Add the roasted beets to the jar and ensure they are submerged.
4. Seal and refrigerate for at least 24 hours before serving.

Air Fryer Kimchi-Style Brussels Sprouts

Prep Time: 15 minutes / Cooking Time: 20 minutes / Servings: 4

Ingredients:
* 200g Brussels sprouts, halved
* 2 tbsp chilli paste (gochujang)
* 1 tbsp grated ginger
* 2 cloves garlic, minced
* 1 tbsp sugar
* Salt to taste

Instructions:
1. Mix chilli paste, ginger, garlic, sugar, and salt in a bowl.
2. Toss Brussels sprouts in the mixture.
3. Air fry at 190°C for 20 minutes or until tender and slightly charred.
4. Store in a jar and refrigerate for at least 12 hours before serving.

Air Fryer Pickled Jalapeños with Agave

Prep Time: 10 minutes / Cooking Time: 10 minutes / Servings: 4

Ingredients:

- 100g jalapeños, sliced
- 200ml apple cider vinegar
- 2 tbsp agave syrup
- 1 tsp salt

Instructions:

1. Air fry the jalapeño slices at 180°C for 10 minutes.
2. In a jar, combine apple cider vinegar, agave syrup, and salt. Stir until dissolved.
3. Add the roasted jalapeños to the jar.
4. Seal and refrigerate for at least 12 hours for flavors to meld.

Air Fryer Roasted Pickled Red Onions

Prep Time: 10 minutes / Cooking Time: 15 minutes / Servings: 4

Ingredients:

- 2 red onions, thinly sliced
- 250ml red wine vinegar
- 2 tbsp sugar
- 1 tsp salt
- 1 bay leaf

Instructions:

1. Air fry the onion slices at 180°C for 15 minutes or until the edges begin to crisp.
2. In a jar, combine red wine vinegar, sugar, salt, and bay leaf. Stir until sugar dissolves.
3. Add the roasted onions, ensuring they're submerged.
4. Seal and refrigerate for at least 24 hours.

Air Fryer Crunchy Kimchi Cabbage Wedges

Prep Time: 20 minutes / Cooking Time: 25 minutes / Servings: 4

Ingredients:

- 1 small cabbage, cut into wedges
- 3 tbsp chilli flakes
- 1 tbsp grated ginger
- 3 cloves garlic, minced
- 2 tbsp soy sauce
- Salt to taste

Instructions:

1. Mix chilli flakes, ginger, garlic, soy sauce, and salt in a bowl.
2. Rub the mixture onto each cabbage wedge, ensuring it's well-coated.
3. Air fry at 190°C for 25 minutes, turning halfway, until the edges are crispy.
4. Store in a container and refrigerate for at least 12 hours for the flavours to deepen.

Air Fryer Rosemary Garlic Potato Wedges

Prep Time: 10 minutes / Cooking Time: 20 minutes / Servings: 4

Ingredients:

- 400g potatoes, cut into wedges
- 2 tbsp olive oil
- 2 cloves garlic, minced
- 1 tbsp fresh rosemary, finely chopped
- Salt and pepper to taste

Instructions:

1. Toss potato wedges with olive oil, garlic, rosemary, salt, and pepper.
2. Air fry at 200°C for 20 minutes, turning halfway, until golden and crispy.

Air Fryer Balsamic Glazed Carrots

Prep Time: 10 minutes / Cooking Time: 15 minutes / Servings: 4

Ingredients:
- 300g baby carrots
- 2 tbsp olive oil
- 3 tbsp balsamic vinegar
- 1 tbsp honey
- Salt to taste

Instructions:
1. Mix olive oil, balsamic vinegar, honey, and salt in a bowl.
2. Coat the baby carrots in the mixture.
3. Air fry at 190°C for 15 minutes or until tender.
4. Drizzle any remaining glaze over the carrots before serving.

Air Fryer Herb-Stuffed Mushrooms

Prep Time: 15 minutes / Cooking Time: 12 minutes / Servings: 4

Ingredients:
- 16 large button mushrooms, stems removed
- 100g cream cheese
- 2 tbsp fresh parsley, chopped
- 1 tbsp fresh chives, chopped
- 1 clove garlic, minced
- Salt and pepper to taste

Instructions:
1. In a bowl, mix cream cheese, parsley, chives, garlic, salt, and pepper.
2. Stuff each mushroom cap with the herb mixture.
3. Air fry at 190°C for 12 minutes or until mushrooms are tender.

Air Fryer Crispy Zucchini Fries

Prep Time: 15 minutes / Cooking Time: 20 minutes / Servings: 4

Ingredients:
- 2 medium zucchinis, cut into sticks
- 100g breadcrumbs
- 50g grated Parmesan cheese
- 1 tsp dried oregano
- Salt and pepper to taste
- 2 eggs, beaten

Instructions:
1. Mix breadcrumbs, Parmesan, oregano, salt, and pepper in a bowl.
2. Dip each zucchini stick into the beaten eggs, then coat with the breadcrumb mixture.
3. Air fry at 200°C for 20 minutes, turning halfway, until golden and crispy.

Air Fryer Roasted Brussels Sprouts with Bacon Bits

Prep Time: 10 minutes / Cooking Time: 18 minutes / Servings: 4

Ingredients:
- 300g Brussels sprouts, halved
- 100g bacon, diced
- 2 tbsp olive oil
- Salt and pepper to taste

Instructions:
1. Toss Brussels sprouts with bacon bits, olive oil, salt, and pepper.
2. Air fry at 190°C for 18 minutes, shaking occasionally, until Brussels sprouts are caramelised and bacon is crispy.

Cauliflower Buffalo Bites

Serves: 4-6 / Prep Time: 10 minutes / Cook time: 10-12 minutes

Ingredients:
- 1 head of cauliflower, cut into small florets
- 64g all-purpose flour
- 1 tsp garlic powder
- 1/2 tsp smoked paprika
- 1/2 tsp salt
- 1/2 tsp black pepper
- 64g buffalo sauce
- 2 tbsp melted butter

Instructions:
1. Preheat the Ninja Dual Zone to Air Fry at 190°C.
2. In a bowl, mix the flour, garlic powder, smoked paprika, salt, and black pepper.
3. Add the cauliflower florets to the bowl and toss until they are coated in the flour mixture.

4. Place the cauliflower in the air fryer basket and Air Fry at 190°C for 10-12 minutes until they are crispy and golden brown.
5. In a separate bowl, mix the buffalo sauce and melted butter.
6. Toss the cooked cauliflower in the buffalo sauce mixture until they are coated.
7. Serve hot.

Mini Cornish Pasties

Serves: 6-8 / Prep Time: 30 minutes / Cook time: 25-30 minutes

Ingredients:
* 320g of all-purpose flour
* 1/2 tsp salt
* 1/2 tsp baking powder
* 64g unsalted butter, chilled and diced
* 64g vegetable shortening, chilled and diced
* 60 ml of cold water
* 1 egg, beaten
* 1 large potato, peeled and diced
* 1 large carrot, peeled and diced
* 1 small onion, peeled and diced
* 128g cooked diced beef
* Salt and pepper, to taste
* 1 tbsp butter, diced

Instructions:
1. Preheat your Ninja Dual Zone to 190°C (190°C) on Air Fry mode.
2. In a large bowl, whisk together flour, salt, and baking powder. Using a pastry blender, cut in butter and shorten until the mixture resembles coarse crumbs.
3. Add cold water and stir until a dough forms. Turn out onto a floured surface and knead for 1-2 minutes until smooth. Divide dough into 8 equal portions and roll each into a ball.
4. In a separate bowl, combine diced potato, carrot, onion, and cooked beef. Season with salt and pepper to taste.
5. On a floured surface, roll each ball of dough into a 5-inch circle. Spoon 32g of the beef and vegetable mixture onto one half of each circle. Dot with butter.
6. Fold the other half of the dough over the filling

and crimp the edges together to seal. Brush the beaten egg over the pasties.
7. Place the pasties in the Ninja Dual Zone on Air Fry mode for 18-20 minutes or until golden brown and crispy.

Pork Dumplings

Serves: 4
Prep Time: 30 minutes / Cook time: 12 minutes

Ingredients:
* 250g ground pork
* 30g finely chopped cabbage
* 2 green onions, finely chopped
* 2 cloves garlic, minced
* 1 tsp grated fresh ginger
* 1 tbsp soy sauce
* 1 tbsp sesame oil
* 1/2 tsp sugar
* 1/4 tsp black pepper
* 24 round dumpling wrappers
* Water, for sealing
* Vegetable oil, for frying

Instructions:
1. Preheat the Ninja Dual Zone Air Fryer to 200°C on zone 1 for 5 minutes.
2. In a bowl, combine the ground pork, chopped cabbage, chopped green onions, minced garlic, grated fresh ginger, soy sauce, sesame oil, sugar, and black pepper. Mix well.
3. Place a small spoonful of the pork filling in the centre of a dumpling wrapper. Moisten the edges of the wrapper with water, then fold it in half and seal the edges, crimping them to create a pleated appearance. Repeat with the remaining wrappers and filling.
4. Place the dumplings in zone 1 of the air fryer, leaving space between them.
5. Cook the pork dumplings at 200°C for 10-12 minutes, or until they are golden brown and cooked through.
6. Once cooked, remove the pork dumplings from the air fryer and let them cool for a minute.

Double Bean Chilli

Serves 8 / Prep Time: 10 minutes / Cook time: 20 minutes

Ingredients

* 2 tbsp rapeseed oil
* 2 medium onions, chopped
* 1 large carrot, chopped
* 2 bell peppers, seeded and chopped
* 2 tsp chipotle paste
* 1 tbsp dried oregano
* 1 tbsp ground coriander
* 1 bay leaf
* 2 (400g) cans tomatoes, crushed
* 4 (400g) cans kidney beans, drained and rinsed
* 1 (400g) can refried beans

Preparation Instructions

1. Heat 1 tablespoon of rapeseed oil in a sauté pan over medium-high heat. Once hot, sauté the onion, carrot, and peppers for about 4 minutes, until just tender.
2. Brush the inside of two oven-safe baking tins with olive oil. Thoroughly combine all the Ingredients.
3. Spoon the mixture into the baking tins and add them to the drawers.
4. Select zone 1 and pair it with "AIR FRY" at 180°C for 20 minutes. Select "MATCH" to duplicate settings across both zones. Press the "START/STOP" button.
5. When zone 1 time reaches 10 minutes, stir the beans, and reinsert the drawers to continue cooking.

Mini Chicken Satay Skewers

Servings: 2 / Prep Time: 7 minutes / Cook Time: 12 minutes

Ingredients

* 450g boneless chicken breast, cut into small pieces
* 3 tablespoons soy sauce
* 2 tablespoons peanut butter
* 1 tablespoon lime juice
* 1 teaspoon curry powder
* 1/2 teaspoon garlic powder
* Wooden skewers, soaked in water

Instructions:

1. Preheat your Ninja Dual Zone Air Fryer to 190°C.
2. To make the marinade, take out a bowl and whisk together the soy sauce, peanut butter, lime juice, curry powder, and garlic powder.
3. Thread the chicken pieces onto the soaked wooden skewers.
4. Place the chicken skewers in a shallow dish and pour the marinade over them, ensuring they are evenly coated.
5. Transfer the skewers to the air fryer drawers.
6. Cook the skewers in the air fryer for 10-12 minutes, or until the chicken is cooked enough to your liking and slightly charred.
7. Remove from the air fryer and serve hot with your favorite dipping sauce.

Sweet Potato Fries

Servings: 2 / Prep Time: 7 minutes / Cook Time: 15 minutes

Ingredients:

* 2 medium sweet potatoes, cut into thin strips
* 2 tablespoons olive oil
* 1 teaspoon paprika
* 1/2 teaspoon garlic powder
* Salt and pepper to taste

Instructions:

1. Preheat your Ninja Dual Zone Air Fryer to 200°C.
2. Toss the sweet potato strips with olive oil, paprika, garlic powder, salt, and pepper until well coated in a bowl.
3. Place the sweet potato strips in the air fryer drawer in a single layer.
4. Cook in the air fryer for 12-15 minutes, or until the sweet potato fries are crispy and golden brown, shaking the basket halfway through to ensure even cooking.
5. Remove from the air fryer and serve hot with your favorite dipping sauce.

Mini Spinach and Feta Quiches

Servings: 2 / Prep Time: 5 minutes / Cook Time: 12 minutes

Ingredients:
- 4 large eggs
- 60ml milk
- 30g chopped spinach
- 113g crumbled feta cheese
- Salt and pepper to taste

Instructions:
1. Preheat your Air Fryer to 190°C.
2. In a bowl, whisk together the eggs and milk. Season with salt and pepper.
3. Divide the chopped spinach and crumbled feta cheese evenly among greased muffin cups.
4. Pour the egg mixture over the spinach and feta in each muffin cup, filling about 3/4 full.
5. Place the muffin cups in the air fryer drawer.
6. Cook in the air fryer for 10-12 minutes, or until the quiches are set and lightly golden.
7. Remove from the air fryer and let cool for a few minutes before serving.

Creamy Beet Salad

Prep Time: 10 minutes + chilling time / Cook time: 40 minutes / Serves 5

Ingredients
- 1kg red beets, peeled, whole
- 1 tbsp extra-virgin olive oil
- 1 tbsp white vinegar
- 1 tsp stone-ground mustard
- 1/2 tsp cumin, ground
- Sea salt and ground black pepper, to taste
- 1 small bulb of garlic
- 1/2 small bunch parsley, roughly chopped
- 1 medium avocado

Preparation Instructions
1. Insert crisper plates in both drawers. Spray the crisper plates with nonstick cooking oil. Place the beets in both drawers of your Ninja Foodi.
2. Select zone 1 and pair it with "AIR FRY" at 200°C for 40 minutes. Select "MATCH" followed by the "START/STOP" button.
3. At the halfway point, turn the beets over to ensure even cooking; wrap the garlic bulb in foil and place it in the zone 1 drawer. Now, reinsert the drawers to resume cooking.
4. In the meantime, place the avocado halves on a cutting board; now, whack the pit with the sharp end of the knife to remove it easily. Use a spoon to scoop avocado flesh; chop your avocado and set it aside.
5. Now, pull or squeeze the roasted garlic cloves out of their skins; mash them with a fork.
6. Let the beets cool and remove the skin. Cut your beets into slices and toss them with the remaining Ingredients, including avocado and roasted garlic. Enjoy!

Butter-Fried Asparagus

Prep Time: 10 minutes / Cook time: 15 minutes / Serves 5

Ingredients
- 1kg asparagus spears, trimmed
- 2 tbsp butter, melted
- 2 garlic cloves, pressed
- 1 tsp dried dill weed
- 1 tsp paprika
- Sea salt and ground black pepper, to taste
- 1/2 lemon, juiced and zested

Preparation Instructions
1. In a mixing dish, toss asparagus with the other Ingredients until well coated in butter and aromatics.
2. Add asparagus to both drawers of your Ninja Foodi (with a crisper plate inserted).
3. Select zone 1 and pair it with "AIR FRY" at 200°C for 15 minutes. Select "MATCH" followed by the "START/STOP" button.
4. At the halfway point, stir the Ingredients to ensure even cooking; reinsert the drawers to resume cooking.
5. Bon appétit!

Chapter 8 Soups and Stews

Air Fryer Moroccan Lentil Soup

Prep Time: 20 minutes / Cooking Time: 40 minutes / Servings: 4

Ingredients:
* 200g green lentils, soaked for 2 hours
* 1 carrot, diced
* 1 onion, chopped
* 2 cloves garlic, minced
* 750ml vegetable broth
* 2 tbsp tomato paste
* 1 tsp ground cumin
* 1 tsp ground turmeric
* 1 tsp paprika
* 2 tbsp olive oil
* Salt and pepper to taste
* Fresh parsley for garnish

Instructions:
1. Toss carrot and onion in olive oil. Air fry at 190°C for 15 minutes.
2. In a pot, sauté garlic in a bit of olive oil until fragrant. Add air-fried vegetables, lentils, vegetable broth, tomato paste, and spices. Simmer for 25 minutes or until lentils are tender.
3. Season with salt and pepper. Garnish with fresh parsley before serving.

Air Fryer Hungarian Mushroom Soup

Prep Time: 15 minutes / Cooking Time: 30 minutes / Servings: 4

Ingredients:
* 300g white mushrooms, sliced
* 1 onion, finely chopped
* 2 cloves garlic, minced
* 500ml vegetable broth
* 200ml sour cream
* 2 tbsp flour
* 2 tbsp olive oil
* 1 tsp paprika
* Salt and pepper to taste
* Fresh dill for garnish

Instructions:
1. Toss mushrooms in olive oil. Air fry at 190°C for 10 minutes.
2. In a pot, sauté onion and garlic until translucent. Add air-fried mushrooms and paprika.
3. Sprinkle flour over the mushroom mixture and stir. Gradually add vegetable broth while stirring. Simmer for 20 minutes.
4. Stir in sour cream and season with salt and pepper. Garnish with fresh dill before serving.

Air Fryer Greek Lemon Chicken Soup (Avgolemono)

Prep Time: 20 minutes / Cooking Time: 30 minutes / Servings: 4

Ingredients:
* 200g chicken breast, diced
* 100g orzo pasta
* 2 eggs, beaten
* Juice of 2 lemons
* 750ml chicken broth
* 2 tbsp olive oil
* Salt and pepper to taste
* Fresh parsley for garnish

Instructions:
1. Toss chicken pieces in olive oil. Air fry at 190°C for 10 minutes or until golden.
2. In a pot, bring chicken broth to a boil. Add orzo pasta and cook until al dente.
3. Add air-fried chicken to the pot and simmer for 5 minutes.
4. Slowly whisk in lemon juice and beaten eggs, stirring continuously until soup thickens slightly.
5. Season with salt and pepper. Garnish with fresh parsley.

Air Fryer French Bouillabaisse

Prep Time: 30 minutes / Cooking Time: 40 minutes / Servings: 4

Ingredients:
* 200g white fish fillets
* 100g mussels, cleaned
* 100g shrimp, peeled
* 1 onion, chopped
* 3 cloves garlic, minced
* 400g canned tomatoes
* 750ml fish stock
* 1 tsp saffron threads
* 2 tbsp olive oil
* 2 tbsp Pernod (optional)
* 1 tbsp orange zest
* Salt and pepper to taste
* Fresh parsley for garnish

Instructions:
1. Toss fish fillets, mussels, and shrimp in olive oil. Air fry at 180°C for 10 minutes.
2. In a pot, sauté onions and garlic in olive oil until translucent. Add tomatoes, fish stock, saffron, Pernod, and orange zest. Bring to a simmer.
3. Add the air-fried seafood to the pot and cook for an additional 20 minutes.
4. Season with salt and pepper. Garnish with fresh parsley.

Air Fryer Brazilian Feijoada

Prep Time: 25 minutes / Cooking Time: 60 minutes / Servings: 4

Ingredients:
* 200g pork shoulder, diced
* 100g chorizo, sliced
* 100g smoked sausage, sliced
* 400g black beans, soaked overnight
* 1 onion, chopped
* 3 cloves garlic, minced
* 750ml chicken stock
* 2 bay leaves
* 2 tbsp olive oil
* Salt and pepper to taste
* Fresh cilantro for garnish

Instructions:
1. Toss pork shoulder, chorizo, and smoked sausage in olive oil. Air fry at 190°C for 15 minutes.
2. In a pot, sauté onions and garlic until fragrant. Add black beans, chicken stock, bay leaves, and air-fried meats.
3. Simmer for 45 minutes or until beans are tender and flavours meld.
4. Season with salt and pepper. Garnish with fresh cilantro.

Air Fryer Japanese Miso Salmon Soup

Prep Time: 20 minutes / Cooking Time: 30 minutes / Servings: 4

Ingredients:
* 200g salmon fillets, diced
* 3 tbsp miso paste
* 750ml dashi stock
* 100g tofu, cubed
* 2 green onions, sliced
* 1 tbsp olive oil
* 2 sheets nori, torn into pieces
* Salt to taste

Instructions:
1. Toss salmon pieces in olive oil. Air fry at 190°C for 10 minutes.
2. In a pot, bring dashi stock to a simmer. Dissolve miso paste in a little bit of the warm stock and then add back to the pot.
3. Add air-fried salmon and tofu to the pot. Cook for 5 minutes.
4. Season with salt if needed. Serve garnished with green onions and nori.

Air Fryer Belgian Beef and Beer Stew

Prep Time: 20 minutes / Cooking Time: 2 hours Servings: 4

Ingredients:
* 300g beef chuck, diced
* 1 onion, chopped
* 2 cloves garlic, minced
* 500ml Belgian beer
* 500ml beef stock

- 2 tbsp brown sugar
- 2 tbsp apple cider vinegar
- 2 tbsp olive oil
- 2 bay leaves
- Salt and pepper to taste

Instructions:

1. Toss beef chunks in olive oil. Air fry at 190°C for 15 minutes.
2. In a pot, sauté onions and garlic until translucent. Add brown sugar and cook until caramelised.
3. Add beer, beef stock, apple cider vinegar, bay leaves, and air-fried beef to the pot. Bring to a simmer.
4. Cook on low heat for 1. 5 hours or until beef is tender. Season with salt and pepper.

Air Fryer Russian Borscht with Beef

Prep Time: 25 minutes / Cooking Time: 45 minutes / Servings: 4

Ingredients:

- 250g beef stew meat, diced
- 3 medium beets, peeled and grated
- 1 carrot, grated
- 1 onion, chopped
- 3 cloves garlic, minced
- 750ml beef broth
- 2 tbsp tomato paste
- 2 tbsp olive oil
- 2 tbsp vinegar
- 2 tsp sugar
- Salt and pepper to taste
- Sour cream and fresh dill for garnish

Instructions:

1. Toss beef pieces in olive oil. Air fry at 190°C for 15 minutes.
2. In a pot, sauté onions, garlic, beets, and carrots until softened. Add tomato paste, vinegar, and sugar.
3. Pour in beef broth, followed by the air-fried beef. Simmer for 30 minutes.
4. Season with salt and pepper. Serve with a dollop of sour cream and a sprinkle of fresh dill.

Air Fryer Peruvian Chicken and Cilantro Soup

Prep Time: 20 minutes / Cooking Time: 40 minutes / Servings: 4

Ingredients:

- 200g chicken breast, diced
- 1 bunch of cilantro, finely chopped
- 1 onion, chopped
- 3 cloves garlic, minced
- 750ml chicken broth
- 100g rice
- 1 bell pepper, diced
- 2 tbsp olive oil
- 1 lime, juiced
- Salt and pepper to taste
- Sliced red chilli for garnish

Instructions:

1. Toss chicken pieces in olive oil. Air fry at 190°C for 10 minutes.
2. In a pot, sauté onions, garlic, and bell pepper until softened. Add rice and chicken broth.
3. Once the rice is halfway cooked, add the air-fried chicken and cilantro. Simmer until chicken is cooked through and rice is tender.
4. Stir in lime juice. Season with salt and pepper. Serve garnished with red chilli slices.

Air Fryer Korean Spicy Tofu and Seafood Stew (Sundubu Jjigae)

Prep Time: 30 minutes / Cooking Time: 30 minutes / Servings: 4

Ingredients:

- 150g mixed seafood (shrimp, mussels, squid)
- 300g soft tofu, cubed
- 2 tbsp gochugaru (Korean red pepper flakes)
- 1 tbsp gochujang (Korean red pepper paste)
- 1 onion, sliced
- 2 cloves garlic, minced
- 750ml seafood broth
- 2 green onions, chopped
- 2 tbsp olive oil
- Salt to taste

Instructions:

1. Toss mixed seafood in olive oil. Air fry at 180°C for 8 minutes.
2. In a pot, sauté onions and garlic until translucent. Add gochugaru and gochujang.
3. Pour in seafood broth and bring to a boil. Add soft tofu and air-fried seafood. Simmer for 20 minutes.
4. Season with salt. Serve garnished with chopped green onions.

Air Fryer Spanish Chorizo and White Bean Stew

Prep Time: 20 minutes / Cooking Time: 40 minutes / Servings: 4

Ingredients:

- 200g chorizo, sliced
- 400g canned white beans, drained
- 1 onion, chopped
- 3 cloves garlic, minced
- 400g canned tomatoes
- 750ml chicken broth
- 2 bay leaves
- 2 tbsp olive oil
- Salt and pepper to taste
- Fresh parsley for garnish

Instructions:

1. Toss chorizo slices in olive oil. Air fry at 190°C for 10 minutes.
2. In a pot, sauté onions and garlic until translucent. Add tomatoes, white beans, chicken broth, bay leaves, and air-fried chorizo.
3. Simmer for 30 minutes. Season with salt and pepper. Garnish with fresh parsley before serving.

Air Fryer Moroccan Lamb and Apricot Stew

Prep Time: 30 minutes / Cooking Time: 50 minutes / Servings: 4

Ingredients:

- 250g lamb shoulder, diced
- 100g dried apricots, chopped
- 1 onion, chopped
- 2 cloves garlic, minced
- 750ml beef broth
- 2 tbsp tomato paste
- 2 tsp ground cumin
- 2 tsp ground coriander
- 1 tsp ground cinnamon
- 2 tbsp olive oil
- Salt and pepper to taste
- Fresh cilantro for garnish

Instructions:

1. Toss lamb pieces in olive oil and spices. Air fry at 190°C for 15 minutes.
2. In a pot, sauté onions and garlic until translucent. Add tomato paste, apricots, and beef broth.
3. Add the air-fried lamb to the pot and simmer for 35 minutes.
4. Season with salt and pepper. Garnish with fresh cilantro.

Air Fryer Filipino Pork Sinigang

Prep Time: 25 minutes / Cooking Time: 40 minutes / Servings: 4

Ingredients:

- 250g pork belly, diced
- 1 radish, sliced
- 1 eggplant, sliced
- 200g string beans, cut into 2-inch lengths
- 1 onion, sliced
- 1 tomato, quartered
- 750ml water
- 1 packet sinigang mix (or substitute with tamarind pulp)
- 2 tbsp olive oil
- Salt to taste
- Green chilli peppers (optional)

Instructions:

1. Toss pork belly pieces in olive oil. Air fry at 190°C for 15 minutes.
2. In a pot, combine water, onion, tomato, and sinigang mix. Bring to a boil.
3. Add the air-fried pork, followed by the vegetables. Simmer until all Ingredients are tender, about 25 minutes.

4. Season with salt. Add green chilli peppers if desired.

Air Fryer Italian Sausage and Bean Soup

Prep Time: 20 minutes / Cooking Time: 35 minutes / Servings: 4

Ingredients:
* 200g Italian sausage, sliced
* 400g canned cannellini beans, drained
* 1 onion, chopped
* 3 cloves garlic, minced
* 400g canned tomatoes
* 750ml chicken broth
* 2 tsp dried basil
* 2 tbsp olive oil
* Salt and pepper to taste
* Grated Parmesan cheese for garnish

Instructions:
1. Toss sausage slices in olive oil. Air fry at 190°C for 10 minutes.
2. In a pot, sauté onions and garlic until fragrant. Add tomatoes, beans, chicken broth, and basil.
3. Add the air-fried sausages and simmer for 25 minutes. Season with salt and pepper.
4. Serve with a sprinkle of Parmesan cheese.

Air Fryer Greek Chicken Lemon Soup (Avgolemono)

Prep Time: 20 minutes / Cooking Time: 30 minutes / Servings: 4

Ingredients:
* 200g chicken breast, diced
* 100g orzo pasta
* 1 lemon, zested and juiced
* 2 eggs, beaten
* 750ml chicken broth
* 2 tbsp olive oil
* Salt and pepper to taste
* Fresh parsley for garnish

Instructions:
1. Toss chicken pieces in olive oil. Air fry at 190°C for 10 minutes.
2. In a pot, bring chicken broth to a boil. Add orzo pasta and cook until al dente.
3. Add the air-fried chicken to the pot and simmer for 5 minutes.
4. In a separate bowl, beat together eggs and lemon juice. Slowly whisk in a ladle of hot soup to temper, then pour the mixture back into the pot while stirring.
5. Season with salt, pepper, and lemon zest. Garnish with fresh parsley.

Chapter 9 Snacks

Air Fryer Filipino Lumpia (Spring Rolls)

Prep Time: 30 minutes / Cooking Time: 12 minutes / Servings: 6

Ingredients:
* 200g ground pork or beef
* 50g carrots, julienned
* 50g green beans, thinly sliced
* 1 onion, finely chopped
* 2 cloves garlic, minced
* Lumpia wrappers
* Salt and pepper to taste

Instructions:
1. Sauté onions and garlic. Add meat and cook until browned. Mix in carrots and green beans. Season with salt and pepper.
2. Place a spoonful of the mixture onto each lumpia wrapper and roll tightly.
3. Air fry at 180°C for 12 minutes or until golden brown.

Air Fryer Middle Eastern Falafel

Prep Time: 20 minutes + soaking time / Cooking Time: 10 minutes / Servings: 4

Ingredients:
* 200g dried chickpeas, soaked overnight
* 1 onion, chopped
* 2 cloves garlic
* 2 tsp ground cumin
* 1 tsp ground coriander
* Fresh parsley, chopped
* Salt to taste
* 1 tsp baking soda

Instructions:
1. Blend soaked chickpeas, onion, garlic, cumin, coriander, parsley, salt, and baking soda until a coarse mixture forms.
2. Form into balls or patties.
3. Air fry at 190°C for 10 minutes or until golden brown.

Air Fryer Indonesian Tempeh Chips

Prep Time: 10 minutes / Cooking Time: 10 minutes / Servings: 4

Ingredients:
* 200g tempeh, sliced thinly
* 2 tbsp soy sauce
* 1 tsp chili powder
* Salt to taste

Instructions:
1. Marinate tempeh slices in soy sauce, chili powder, and salt for 10 minutes.
2. Air fry at 190°C for 10 minutes or until crispy.

Air Fryer South African Biltong

Prep Time: 10 minutes + marination time / Cooking Time: 3 hours at low temp / Servings: 4

Ingredients:
* 500g beef or game meat, cut into strips
* 50ml apple cider vinegar
* 2 tbsp coarse salt
* 1 tbsp coriander seeds, crushed
* 1 tsp black pepper

Instructions:
1. Marinate meat strips in vinegar, salt, coriander seeds, and black pepper for 3 hours.
2. Air fry at 70°C for 3 hours or until dried but still slightly soft.

Air Fryer Turkish Sigara Böreği (Cheese Rolls)

Prep Time: 20 minutes / Cooking Time: 10 minutes / Servings: 6

Ingredients:
* 12 sheets phyllo pastry
* 150g feta cheese, crumbled
* 2 tbsp fresh parsley, chopped
* 50ml olive oil or melted butter

Instructions:
1. Mix feta cheese and parsley.
2. Cut each phyllo sheet into 3 strips. Place a spoonful of cheese mixture at one end and roll into a cigar shape.
3. Brush with olive oil or butter.
4. Air fry at 180°C for 10 minutes or until golden.

Air Fryer Brazilian Coxinha (Chicken Croquettes)

Prep Time: 30 minutes / Cooking Time: 15 minutes / Servings: 6

Ingredients:
* 200g chicken breast, cooked and shredded
* 100g cream cheese
* 250g flour
* 500ml chicken broth
* 1 onion, finely chopped
* 2 cloves garlic, minced
* Salt and pepper to taste

Instructions:
1. Sauté onions and garlic. Add chicken, cream cheese, salt, and pepper.
2. In a separate pot, bring chicken broth to a boil and slowly add flour, stirring continuously until a dough forms.
3. Take a small portion of dough, flatten, fill with chicken mixture, and shape into a drumstick form.
4. Air fry at 190°C for 15 minutes or until golden brown.

Air Fryer Japanese Korokke (Potato Croquettes)

Prep Time: 25 minutes / Cooking Time: 15 minutes / Servings: 4

Ingredients:
* 200g potatoes, boiled and mashed
* 100g ground beef or pork
* 1 onion, chopped
* Salt and pepper to taste
* 50g flour
* 1 egg, beaten
* 100g breadcrumbs

Instructions:
1. Sauté onions and meat until cooked. Mix with mashed potatoes, salt, and pepper.
2. Form into oval shapes, coat with flour, dip in beaten egg, and then coat with breadcrumbs.
3. Air fry at 190°C for 15 minutes or until golden.

Air Fryer Greek Spanakopita (Spinach Pie)

Prep Time: 30 minutes / Cooking Time: 12 minutes / Servings: 6

Ingredients:
* 200g spinach, chopped
* 150g feta cheese, crumbled
* 1 onion, finely chopped
* 2 cloves garlic, minced
* 12 sheets phyllo pastry
* 100ml olive oil
* Salt and pepper to taste

Instructions:
1. Sauté onions, garlic, and spinach. Mix with feta, salt, and pepper.
2. Place a spoonful of the mixture onto a phyllo sheet, fold to form a triangle, and brush with olive oil.
3. Air fry at 180°C for 12 minutes or until golden.

Air Fryer Indian Samosas

Prep Time: 40 minutes / Cooking Time: 15 minutes / Servings: 6

Ingredients:
* 250g flour
* 100ml water
* 200g potatoes, boiled and mashed
* 100g peas
* 1 onion, chopped
* 2 tsp curry powder
* Salt to taste

Instructions:
1. Make a dough with flour and water. Let rest.
2. Sauté onions, add peas, potatoes, curry powder, and salt.
3. Roll out dough, cut circles, fill with mixture,

and fold into a triangle.

4. Air fry at 190°C for 15 minutes or until golden.

Air Fryer Spanish Patatas Bravas

Prep Time: 10 minutes / Cooking Time: 20 minutes / Servings: 4

Ingredients:
* 300g potatoes, diced
* 2 tbsp olive oil
* 100ml tomato sauce
* 1 tsp smoked paprika
* 1 tsp chili powder
* Salt to taste

Instructions:
1. Toss potatoes in olive oil, salt, and smoked paprika.
2. Air fry at 200°C for 20 minutes or until crispy.
3. Warm tomato sauce, mix in chili powder, and pour over potatoes.

Air Fryer Italian Arancini (Rice Balls)

Prep Time: 30 minutes / Cooking Time: 15 minutes / Servings: 6

Ingredients:
* 300g cooked risotto rice
* 100g mozzarella cheese, cubed
* 50g breadcrumbs
* 2 eggs, beaten
* Salt and pepper to taste
* 1 tsp dried oregano

Instructions:
1. Take a spoonful of risotto rice, place a cheese cube in the centre, and shape into a ball.
2. Dip each ball in beaten eggs, coat with breadcrumbs, and season with salt, pepper, and oregano.
3. Air fry at 190°C for 15 minutes or until golden brown.

Air Fryer French Ratatouille Stuffed Mushrooms

Prep Time: 20 minutes / Cooking Time: 10 minutes / Servings: 4

Ingredients:
* 8 large mushrooms, stems removed
* 50g zucchini, finely diced
* 50g bell peppers, finely diced
* 50g eggplant, finely diced
* 2 cloves garlic, minced
* 2 tbsp olive oil
* Salt and pepper to taste

Instructions:
1. Sauté zucchini, bell peppers, eggplant, and garlic in olive oil until tender. Season with salt and pepper.
2. Fill each mushroom cap with the vegetable mixture.
3. Air fry at 180°C for 10 minutes or until mushrooms are cooked.

Air Fryer Korean Tteokbokki (Spicy Rice Cakes)

Prep Time: 10 minutes / Cooking Time: 10 minutes / Servings: 4

Ingredients:
* 200g rice cakes
* 50ml gochujang (Korean red chili paste)
* 1 tbsp soy sauce
* 1 tbsp sugar
* 2 green onions, chopped
* 150ml water

Instructions:
1. In a bowl, mix gochujang, soy sauce, sugar, and water to create the sauce.
2. Toss rice cakes in the sauce.
3. Air fry at 180°C for 10 minutes or until slightly crispy.
4. Garnish with green onions.

Air Fryer American Buffalo Cauliflower Bites

Prep Time: 15 minutes / Cooking Time: 15 minutes / Servings: 4

Ingredients:
* 300g cauliflower florets
* 100ml hot sauce

- 2 tbsp butter, melted
- 1 tsp garlic powder
- Salt to taste
- 50g breadcrumbs

Instructions:

1. Mix hot sauce, melted butter, garlic powder, and salt in a bowl.
2. Toss cauliflower florets in the sauce, then coat with breadcrumbs.
3. Air fry at 190°C for 15 minutes or until crispy.

Air Fryer Peruvian Tequeños (Cheese Sticks)

Prep Time: 20 minutes / Cooking Time: 10 minutes / Servings: 6

Ingredients:

- 12 wonton wrappers
- 150g white cheese, cut into sticks
- 1 egg, beaten

Instructions:

1. Place a cheese stick on the edge of a wonton wrapper, roll tightly, and seal edges with beaten egg.
2. Air fry at 190°C for 10 minutes or until golden brown.

Griddled Aubergine Rounds

Prep Time: 10 minutes / Cook time: 15 minutes / Serves 5

Ingredients

- 3 medium aubergines, cut into 1cm-thick slices
- 1 tbsp olive oil
- Sea salt and ground black pepper, to taste
- 1 tsp cayenne pepper
- 1 tsp dried dill weed
- 1/2 tsp sumac
- 200g Parmesan cheese, grated

Preparation Instructions

1. Insert crisper plates in both drawers. Spray the crisper plates with nonstick cooking oil.
2. Toss aubergines with olive oil, salt, black pepper, cayenne pepper, dill, and sumac. Arrange the aubergine rounds in both drawers

of your Ninja Foodi.

3. Select zone 1 and pair it with "AIR FRY" at 190°C for 15 minutes. Select "MATCH" followed by the "START/STOP" button.
4. At the halfway point, turn aubergine rounds over and top them with cheese; reinsert the drawers to resume cooking.
5. Bon appétit!

Courgette Fritters

Prep Time: 10 minutes / Cook time: 20 minutes / Serves 5

Ingredients

- 400g courgette, grated
- 200g plain flour
- 2 medium eggs, beaten
- 1 small onion, chopped
- 1/2 lemon, zested
- 50g Parmesan cheese, grated
- 1/2 tsp dried dill
- Sea salt and ground black pepper, to taste
- 1 tsp paprika
- 1 tsp dried oregano
- 1 tbsp olive oil

Preparation Instructions

1. Insert crisper plates in both drawers. Spray the crisper plates with nonstick cooking oil.
2. Toss the courgette with 1 teaspoon of coarse sea salt in a colander; let it sit for about 15 minutes; after that, squeeze out the excess moisture using tea towels.
3. Thoroughly combine grated courgette with the remaining Ingredients. Shape the mixture into small patties and arrange them in both drawers.
4. Select zone 1 and pair it with "AIR FRY" at 190°C for 20 minutes. Select "MATCH" followed by the "START/STOP" button.
5. At the halfway point, turn the courgette fritters over, and reinsert the drawers to resume cooking.
6. Bon appétit!

Beignets

Serves: 6 / Prep Time: 20 minutes / Cook time: 8 minutes

Ingredients:
- For the dough:
- 250g all-purpose flour
- 2 tsp baking powder
- 1/2 tsp salt
- 1 tbsp granulated sugar
- 120ml milk
- 1 egg, beaten
- 1 tbsp unsalted butter, melted
- Vegetable oil, for frying
- Powdered sugar, for dusting

Instructions:
1. In a large mixing bowl, whisk together flour, baking powder, salt, and sugar.
2. In a separate bowl, combine milk, beaten egg, and melted butter.
3. Gradually pour wet Ingredients into the dry mixture and stir to combine. Mix until dough forms a smooth and sticky texture.
4. Cover the bowl with a clean kitchen towel and let it rest for 30 minutes.
5. Preheat the Ninja Dual Zone Air Fryer to 175°C.
6. Pour vegetable oil into the Air Fryer basket and preheat for 2 minutes.
7. Using a small ice cream scoop or spoon, scoop dough into round balls and gently drop into the hot oil.
8. Fry for about 4 minutes or until beignets are golden brown.
9. Use a slotted spoon to remove beignets and place them on a paper towel-lined plate to cool.

Blueberry Hand Pies

Serves: 4 / Prep Time: 15 minutes / Cook time: 12 minutes

Ingredients:
- 200g fresh blueberries
- 50g granulated sugar
- 1 tbsp cornstarch
- 1 tsp lemon juice
- 8 small pre-made pie crusts
- 2 tbsp unsalted butter, melted
- Icing sugar, for dusting

Instructions:
1. Preheat the Ninja Dual Zone Air Fryer to 190°C in zone 1 for 5 minutes.
2. In a bowl, combine the fresh blueberries, granulated sugar, cornstarch, and lemon juice. Gently mix until the blueberries are coated.
3. Roll out the pie crusts and cut them into smaller circles to fit your silicone muffin cups.
4. Press each pie crust circle into a silicone muffin cup, forming a small pie shell.
5. Fill each pie shell with the blueberry mixture, dividing it evenly among the cups.
6. Brush the melted butter over the top of each hand pie.
7. Place the hand pies in zone 1 of the air fryer, leaving space between them.
8. Cook the pies at 190°C for 10-12 minutes, or until the crust is golden brown and the blueberries are bubbling.
9. Once cooked, remove the hand pies from the air fryer and let them cool for a minute.

Lemon Bars

Serves: 4 / Prep Time: 15 minutes / Cook time: 25 minutes

Ingredients:
- 120g unsalted butter, softened
- 50g powdered sugar
- 160g all-purpose flour
- 2 large eggs
- 200g granulated sugar
- 30g all-purpose flour
- 1/2 tsp baking powder
- Zest of 1 lemon
- Juice of 1 lemon
- Powdered sugar, for dusting

Instructions:
1. Preheat the Ninja Dual Zone Air Fryer to 180°C on zone 1 for 5 minutes.
2. In a bowl, cream together the softened butter and powdered sugar until light and fluffy.
3. Add the flour and mix until crumbly.

4. Press the mixture evenly into the bottom of a greased baking dish or silicone baking mould.
5. In another bowl, whisk together the eggs, granulated sugar, flour, baking powder, lemon zest, and lemon juice until well combined.
6. Pour the lemon mixture over the crust in the baking dish or mould.
7. Place the baking dish or mould in zone 1 of the air fryer and cook at 180°C for 25 minutes or until the edges are golden brown and the centre is set.
8. Once cooked, remove the lemon bars from the air fryer and let them cool completely.

Mozzarella Sticks

Prep Time: 10 minutes / Cook time: 8 minutes / Serves 6

Ingredients
* 400g block firm mozzarella cheese, cut into 1cm-thick finger-length strips
* 100g all-purpose flour
* 1 medium egg
* 150g breadcrumbs
* 1 tsp garlic granules
* 1 tsp dried parsley flakes
* Sea salt and cayenne pepper, to your liking
* 1 tbsp olive oil

Preparation Instructions
1. Insert crisper plates in both drawers. Spray the crisper plates with nonstick cooking oil.
2. Next, set up your breading station. Place all-purpose flour in a shallow dish. In a separate dish, whisk the egg. Lastly, thoroughly combine the breadcrumbs with garlic granules, parsley flakes, salt, and cayenne pepper in a third dish.
3. Start by dredging mozzarella sticks in the flour; then, dip them into the egg. Press mozzarella sticks into the breadcrumb mixture.
4. Brush breaded mozzarella sticks with olive oil and arrange them in both drawers.
5. Select zone 1 and pair it with "AIR FRY" at 190°C for 8 minutes. Select "MATCH" followed by the "START/STOP" button.
6. At the halfway point, turn the mozzarella sticks over to ensure even cooking; reinsert the drawers to resume cooking.
7. Serve mozzarella sticks with a dipping sauce of your choice, and enjoy!
8. Bon appétit!

Chapter 10 Desserts

Air Fryer Turkish Baklava Bites

Prep Time: 30 minutes / Cooking Time: 15 minutes / Servings: 20 bites

Ingredients:
* 10 sheets of phyllo dough
* 150g mixed nuts (pistachios, walnuts, almonds), finely chopped
* 100g melted butter
* 150g sugar
* 150ml water
* 1 tsp lemon juice

Instructions:
1. Brush each phyllo sheet with butter and stack them. Cut into small squares.
2. Place a spoonful of nuts in the centre of each square and fold to form a triangle.
3. Air fry at 180°C for 15 minutes or until golden brown.
4. Meanwhile, make a syrup by boiling sugar, water, and lemon juice. Pour over the warm baklava bites.

Air Fryer Japanese Mochi Donuts

Prep Time: 25 minutes / Cooking Time: 10 minutes / Servings: 10 donuts

Ingredients:
* 200g glutinous rice flour
* 100g sugar
* 200ml water
* Food colouring (optional)
* Sugar glaze or powdered sugar for coating

Instructions:
1. Mix rice flour, sugar, and water until a smooth batter forms. Add food colouring if desired.
2. Pipe the batter into ring shapes onto parchment paper.
3. Air fry at 180°C for 10 minutes until slightly golden.
4. Coat with sugar glaze or powdered sugar while still warm.

Air Fryer Italian Cannoli Cones

Prep Time: 30 minutes / Cooking Time: 8 minutes / Servings: 8 cannoli

Ingredients:
* 8 small tortilla wraps
* 200g ricotta cheese
* 50g powdered sugar
* 50g mini chocolate chips
* Zest of 1 lemon
* Powdered sugar for dusting

Instructions:
1. Shape tortilla wraps into cone shapes and secure with a toothpick.
2. Air fry at 180°C for 8 minutes until crisp.
3. Mix ricotta, powdered sugar, chocolate chips, and lemon zest.
4. Once the cones are cooled, fill them with the ricotta mixture.
5. Dust with powdered sugar.

Air Fryer French Crème Brûlée Bowls

Prep Time: 20 minutes / Cooking Time: 15 minutes / Servings: 6 bowls

Ingredients:
* 500ml heavy cream
* 6 egg yolks
* 100g sugar
* 1 tsp vanilla extract
* Additional sugar for caramelising

Instructions:
1. Whisk egg yolks, sugar, and vanilla. Gradually add in heavy cream.
2. Pour into small ramekins.
3. Air fry at 150°C for 15 minutes until set but still jiggly.
4. Cool, then sprinkle sugar on top and caramelise with a torch.

Air Fryer Spanish Churro Bites

Prep Time: 20 minutes / Cooking Time: 8 minutes / Servings: 20 bites

Ingredients:
* 200ml water
* 50g butter
* 150g all-purpose flour
* 2 eggs
* Sugar and cinnamon mix for coating
* Melted chocolate for dipping

Instructions:
1. Boil water and butter. Remove from heat and stir in flour until a dough forms.
2. Once cooled slightly, add eggs one at a time.
3. Pipe dough into small bite-sized pieces.
4. Air fry at 190°C for 8 minutes or until golden.
5. Toss in sugar and cinnamon mix.

Air Fryer Australian Lamingtons

Prep Time: 20 minutes / Cooking Time: 15 minutes / Servings: 12 pieces

Ingredients:
* 200g sponge cake, pre-made
* 200g chocolate sauce
* 100g desiccated coconut

Instructions:
1. Cut the sponge cake into squares.
2. Dip each piece in chocolate sauce, then roll in desiccated coconut.
3. Air fry at 160°C for 15 minutes until lightly crispy.

Air Fryer German Apple Fritters

Prep Time: 20 minutes / Cooking Time: 10 minutes / Servings: 8 fritters

Ingredients:
* 2 apples, sliced into rings
* 100g all-purpose flour
* 1 egg
* 100ml milk
* Powdered sugar for dusting

Instructions:
1. Mix flour, egg, and milk to form a smooth batter.
2. Dip apple rings into the batter.
3. Air fry at 180°C for 10 minutes, flipping halfway.
4. Dust with powdered sugar.

Air Fryer Russian Syrniki (Cheese Pancakes)

Prep Time: 15 minutes / Cooking Time: 10 minutes / Servings: 8 pancakes

Ingredients:
* 200g cottage cheese
* 1 egg
* 50g sugar
* 100g all-purpose flour
* 1 tsp baking powder

Instructions:
1. Mix all Ingredients to form a dough.
2. Shape into small pancakes.
3. Air fry at 180°C for 10 minutes, flipping halfway.

Air Fryer Moroccan Almond Briouats

Prep Time: 25 minutes / Cooking Time: 10 minutes / Servings: 12 pastries

Ingredients:
* 12 phyllo dough sheets
* 150g ground almonds
* 50g sugar
* 1 tsp cinnamon
* 100g melted butter

Instructions:
1. Mix almonds, sugar, and cinnamon.
2. Place a spoonful of the almond mix on each phyllo sheet and fold into triangles.
3. Brush with melted butter.
4. Air fry at 180°C for 10 minutes until golden.

Air Fryer Peruvian Picarones (Sweet Potato Donuts)

Prep Time: 30 minutes (plus resting) / Cooking Time: 10 minutes / Servings: 10 donuts

Ingredients:
* 100g mashed sweet potato
* 100g mashed squash

- 200g all-purpose flour
- 1 tsp yeast
- 100g brown sugar
- 200ml water

Instructions:

1. Mix mashed sweet potato, squash, flour, and yeast to form a dough.
2. Let it rest for 2 hours.
3. Shape dough into ring donuts.
4. Air fry at 190°C for 10 minutes.
5. Make a syrup with brown sugar and water, then drizzle over warm donuts.

Air Fryer Polish Faworki (Angel Wings)

Prep Time: 30 minutes / Cooking Time: 10 minutes / Servings: 20 pastries

Ingredients:

- 200g all-purpose flour
- 50g powdered sugar
- 50g butter
- 3 egg yolks
- 50ml sour cream
- Powdered sugar for dusting

Instructions:

1. Mix all Ingredients to form a dough.
2. Roll out thinly and cut into strips, then twist into 'wing' shapes.
3. Air fry at 180°C for 10 minutes until golden.
4. Dust with powdered sugar.

Air Fryer Chinese Sesame Balls

Prep Time: 25 minutes / Cooking Time: 12 minutes / Servings: 10 balls

Ingredients:

- 200g glutinous rice flour
- 100g red bean paste
- 100g white sesame seeds
- 100ml water

Instructions:

1. Mix rice flour with water to form a dough.
2. Divide into balls and fill each with a spoonful of red bean paste.
3. Roll in sesame seeds.

4. Air fry at 180°C for 12 minutes until golden and crispy.

Air Fryer Egyptian Basbousa (Semolina Cake)

Prep Time: 20 minutes / Cooking Time: 15 minutes / Servings: 8 pieces

Ingredients:

- 200g semolina
- 100g sugar
- 100g plain yoghourt
- 1 tsp baking powder
- 50g desiccated coconut
- Almonds for garnish
- 100g sugar and 100ml water for syrup

Instructions:

1. Mix semolina, sugar, yoghurt, baking powder, and coconut to form a batter.
2. Spread in a dish and score into diamond shapes, placing an almond on each.
3. Air fry at 170°C for 15 minutes.
4. Boil sugar and water to make a syrup and pour over the warm cake.

Air Fryer Belgian Liege Waffles

Prep Time: 30 minutes (plus resting) Cooking Time: 10 minutes / Servings: 8 waffles

Ingredients:

- 250g all-purpose flour
- 1 tsp yeast
- 100ml warm milk
- 1 egg
- 100g butter
- 100g pearl sugar

Instructions:

1. Mix flour, yeast, milk, and egg to form a dough.
2. Incorporate butter and let it rest for 1 hour.
3. Fold in pearl sugar and shape into waffles.
4. Air fry at 190°C for 10 minutes until golden.

Prep Time: 20 minutes / Cooking Time: 8 minutes / Servings: 15 truffles

Ingredients:

- 1 can condensed milk
- 2 tbsp cocoa powder

- 2 tbsp butter
- Chocolate sprinkles for rolling

Instructions:
1. Mix condensed milk, cocoa, and butter in a pan until thickened.
2. Let it cool, then shape into balls.
3. Roll in chocolate sprinkles.
4. Air fry at 160°C for 8 minutes for a slightly crusty exterior.

Cinnamon Sugar Doughnut Holes

Serves: 6 / Prep Time: 20 minutes / Cook time: 8 minutes

Ingredients:
- For the dough:
- 250g all-purpose flour
- 1 tsp baking powder
- 1/2 tsp salt
- 120g granulated sugar
- 100ml milk
- 1 egg, beaten
- 1 tsp vanilla extract
- 60g unsalted butter, melted
- Vegetable oil, for frying
- For the coating:
- 120g granulated sugar
- 1 tsp ground cinnamon

Instructions:
1. In a large mixing bowl, whisk together flour, baking powder, salt, and sugar.
2. In a separate bowl, combine milk, beaten egg, vanilla extract, and melted butter.
3. Gradually pour wet Ingredients into the dry mixture and stir to combine. Mix until dough forms a smooth and sticky texture.
4. Cover the bowl with a clean kitchen towel and let it rest for 30 minutes.
5. Preheat the Ninja Dual Zone Air Fryer to 175°C.
6. Pour vegetable oil into the Air Fryer basket and preheat for 2 minutes.
7. Using a small ice cream scoop or spoon, scoop dough into round balls and gently drop into the hot oil.

8. Fry for about 4 minutes or until doughnut holes are golden brown.
9. In a separate bowl, mix sugar and cinnamon together for the coating.
10. Use a slotted spoon to remove doughnut holes and immediately coat them in the cinnamon sugar mixture.
11. Serve warm.

Roasted Beet Chips with Feta Cheese Dip

Serves: 2 / Prep Time: 10 minutes / Cook time: 20 minutes

Ingredients:
- For the beet chips:
- 2 medium-sized beets
- 1 tbsp olive oil
- Sea salt and black pepper, to taste
- For the feta cheese dip:
- 50g feta cheese
- 2 tbsp Greek yoghurt
- 1 tbsp lemon juice
- 1 tbsp chopped fresh dill
- 1 small garlic clove, minced
- Sea salt and black pepper, to taste

Instructions:
1. Preheat the Ninja Dual Zone Air Fryer to 180°C using the "ROAST" function on zone 2.
2. Wash and peel the beets, and slice them into thin rounds.
3. In a bowl, toss the beet slices with olive oil, salt, and pepper.
4. Arrange the beet slices on the crisper plate on zone 2 of the air fryer, making sure not to overcrowd the plate.
5. Roast the beet slices for 20 minutes, flipping them halfway through the Cooking Time, until crispy and golden brown.
6. While the beets are roasting, prepare the feta cheese dip by combining all the dip Ingredients in a small bowl and mixing until smooth.

Printed in Great Britain
by Amazon